DON'T MESS UP YOUR RICE

GALLERY BOOKS UK
London · New York · Amsterdam/Antwerp · Sydney/Melbourne · Toronto · New Delhi

70 Recipes
to Impress
Uncle Roger

DON'T MESS UP YOUR RICE

NIGEL NG
with Jenn Garbee
Photography by Jennifer Chong
Foreword by Gordon Ramsay

FOR SABRINA.
TO MANY MORE
DINNERS
TOGETHER.

First published in the United States by Simon Element,
an imprint of Simon & Schuster, LLC, 2026

First published in Great Britain by Simon & Schuster UK Ltd, 2026

1 3 5 7 9 10 8 6 4 2

Simon & Schuster UK Ltd
7th Floor
199 Bishopsgate
London
EC2M 3TY

www.simonandschuster.co.uk
www.simonandschuster.com.au
www.simonandschuster.co.in

Simon & Schuster Australia, Sydney
Simon & Schuster India, New Delhi

The authorised representative in the EEA is Simon & Schuster Netherlands BV, Herculesplein 96, 3584 AA Utrecht, Netherlands. info@simonandschuster.nl

A CIP catalogue record for this book is available from the British Library

Hardback ISBN: 978-1-3985-5453-5
eBook ISBN: 978-1-3985-5454-2

Food Stylist: Natalie Drobny
Prop Stylist: Ruth Kim
Photo Assistant: David Peng
Food Styling Assistant: Paige Arnett
Prop Styling Assistant: Tokyo Lucy

Printed in China

MIX
Paper | Supporting responsible forestry
FSC® C144853

UNCLE ROGER'S KITCHEN

FRY RICE

(FUIYOH!)

THE ONLY VEGETABLE UNCLE ROGER EAT

ASIAN AMERICAN

THE WORST RECIPES IN THIS BOOK

UNCLE ROGER FAVORITE RECIPES IN WHOLE WORLD

(FROM MY MUM!)

NOODLES

CURRIES

OTHER DISHES THAT UNCLE ROGER CRAVES

SWEETS

FOREWORD

In 2020, I was deep in the forests of Indonesia. After a tiring afternoon of working with local farmers and cooking a feast for dignitaries, I had one more trick up my sleeve: cooking a Nasi Goreng. I was exhausted, but my producer convinced me it would make the internet go crazy. Just before a massive rainstorm rolled in, we shot that beautiful fried-rice dish in the middle of a gorgeous field. The rice was crispy, the egg was perfect, and it looked absolutely delicious. I was proud of myself, but little did I know the global impact that dish would have—or the havoc it would wreak thanks to a certain YouTuber named Uncle Roger.

When my daughter Tilly first showed me the video of Uncle Roger reviewing my cooking, I had a quick laugh and carried on. But soon my kids, my friends, and my fellow chefs were messaging me, congratulating me on my new "Uncle title." I had no idea what an honor had been bestowed upon me! It was then I realized that Uncle Roger was a friend in the culinary field, not a foe.

In the years that followed, I cooked a few dishes that cost me my crown (we don't talk about the grilled cheese). But it wasn't until I finally met Nigel while filming in Brighton in 2022 that he became a real friend. It was there

I truly learned about his passion for his character, his love for Asian cuisine, and our mutual displeasure with a certain *other* British chef. Our day together was full of laughs, mutual respect, and a proper cook-off to reclaim my status.

Since then, we've had our online battles, but I've watched Nigel's growth with immense respect. From his global comedy specials to texting me recipes for my thoughts, Nigel has become an unexpected powerhouse. Throughout this book—in between a few digs at me (Nigel, I know how to melt cheese now)—you'll find incredible dishes from across Asia and America. Given his world tours, he's been able to dive headfirst into perfecting these recipes, with a few Aunties, Nieces, and even his mum helping him along the way.

If you love Asian cuisine, you are going to love this cookbook. These are fantastic recipes, and hopefully I can guarantee you one thing: if you cook these correctly, you won't get slated by a YouTuber. Go enjoy—trust me, you're going to love it.

—GORDON RAMSAY

INTRODUCTION

Good Morning

WOW, I'M WRITING A COOKBOOK.

And I've left writing this introduction all the way to the last minute. Maybe it's because compared to the recipes, this introduction feels like it requires a lot more introspection to get right. It's no longer measurements and ingredients and cooking steps. I had to think about how food, comedy, and an overdose of video editing got me to where I am today.

Before creating Uncle Roger, I had been doing the standup circuit for nearly ten years. Then Covid hit. Live shows were canceled, and like everybody else, I was stuck at home. Two weeks turned into four weeks, then another month and another. I started hosting a weekly podcast (at the peak of the pandemic you either had Covid or you had a podcast). A fan of the podcast sent me a video . . . the BBC Food egg fried rice video that started it all.

I was genuinely shocked watching this BBC Food host butcher something that was second nature to me. It was a shambles! I was born and raised in Malaysia, and like so many other Asian families, we all grew up with rice; it was intuitive to us: how to cook it, cook with it, eat it. Everything about the video was beyond bad, except the bright, cheerful host. Toward the end when she poured the cooked rice into a sieve and then ran the rice under tap water, I watched with incredulity. This was the most anemic-looking fried rice I'd ever seen. Until then, I thought fried rice was pretty hard to mess up.

Uncle Roger was born out of that genuine moment. I had in mind this middle-aged Asian boomer with a know-it-all attitude, inspired by my loud-mouthed relatives back home. A character with a name that is out of fashion, very "safe," and with a heavy infusion of Britishness—not surprising, given the colonial roots of so much of Southeast Asia. A name much like Nigel. I had an orange polo ready to go. It was an easy costume for a character sketch, but it was also in keeping with what my dad would wear. A polo shirt had a collar, which meant it was respectable, and because it was the classic short-sleeve version, it was practical as well (at least in the hot climate where I grew up). I thought about how this character, the Asian uncle we all know, would feel about the butchering of something as simple as fried rice. I drew the curtains, turned on my ring light, clipped on my mic, hit the big red button on the front of the camera . . . and took a deep breath.

"Hallo, my name is Uncle Roger."

Here I am today, six years later writing the introduction to my cookbook—Uncle Roger's cookbook. It's something I never could have imagined that day when I took the leap with this new comedic character. Over the years, Uncle Roger embodied my own frustrations as a Malaysian living in Britain. In Malaysia, eating out was not just cheap and convenient, the food was incredible. The hawker centers had stalls and stalls of different, delicious foods to order with big, bold flavors and aromas. The Maggi goreng you could get at 3:00 a.m. could be as satisfying as a three-star Michelin meal.

I have a deep connection to Southeast Asian food, which you'll see in the recipes in this cookbook. My mom would bring me to one pan mee stall every day after primary school, me sitting there in my uniform (white short-sleeved shirt and navy shorts), feet dangling in midair and slurping away at my noodles in their melamine bowls. And so began my lifelong love for noodles in broth. It's no wonder that so many immigrants learn to make the food they grew up eating only when they're away from it. It helps remind us of a place where we belonged, and that we loved. A place that is part of who we are.

I won't go into my "bad" food experiences outside of Southeast Asia, especially when I lived in London or now, Los Angeles. Uncle Roger has already shared many of my thoughts there with all of you. And there is an

SEOUL
Good Morning

JACKFRUIT
PACKED BY:
THAI BANANA
NET WT.
COUNT
THAI BANANAS

enormous amount of incredible food from all cultures available abroad, often presented in an entirely new way. I appreciate those renditions from chefs and home cooks alike, even if Uncle Roger does not. But I hope in this cookbook you'll see more than just Uncle Roger ripping apart bad recipes. Both he and I have a genuine love for Asian culture and Asian food, and for the vast number of things those two phrases encompass. It would be impossible for anyone to say they are the expert on every single aspect of Asian cooking (unless your name is Uncle Roger). Just working on this book, I've learned so much and changed some of my views about the challenges and realities that home cooks face in re-creating truly "authentic" dishes outside their homelands. I do think we got as close as we could, but I know some of you are going to tell Uncle Roger his version is all wrong. (I look forward to the challenge. Tag me @mrnigelng and tell me how you or your family make these dishes differently.) And I happen to think the recipes are all fantastic, even if I could only scratch the surface in a single book on Asian cooking. (Uncle Roger would not agree with me about the Chilli Jam [page 120], but as long as you don't use it in any Asian dish, it's a solid British-style jam.) So many recipes we had to scrap, as we ran out of room.

Ultimately, the people I really have to thank are you, the fans of Uncle Roger. Over the years I've seen you all coming out to my live shows, eating at my restaurants, commenting, and tagging me on socials. As someone who remembers the struggle in obscurity during the decade I was grinding it out on the standup circuit, I truly appreciate it all. It's been such a privilege growing with you.

Now, it's time to pass the torch to my grumpy uncle to handle things from this page forward.

(Haiyaa, enough with Nephew Nigel sob story. Niece and nephew, are you ready to cook some good food?)

Three Ladies Brand
BA CÔ GÁI
PRODUCT OF THAILAND

UNCLE ROGER'S KITCHEN

WE DON'T USE A DISHWASHER
IN THIS HOUSE!

Tools Asian People Have in Their Kitchen

Only four kitchen tool Asian people need to make the most delicious food in whole world: rice cooker, wok, stove, and mortar and pestle. Everything else just extras company sell to convince people to waste their money.

Rice cooker need no explanation. Every Asian baby learn to cook rice after speak first words. (Go to page 32 if you are not Asian and Uncle Roger tell you how.)

Wok must be seasoned and NEVER nonstick! No other option.

Wok stove always best. Indoor, outdoor, portable, nobody care because they know you make the best fry rice (see page 38) like Uncle Roger. Western stove OK and it what even Uncle Roger have to use where I live. Take a little longer to heat up your wok. Even tiny portable stove for college dorm work if that all you have. Most college dorm will tell you not to bring cooking appliance because of fire hazard. Uncle Roger say ignore that. College food terrible, portable stove your only hope.

And for pounding . . . need a big, tough **mortar and pestle.** Granite or something that can handle a constant workout. One mortar and pestle a must, two even better. If have room in your kitchen, get a Thai clay mortar and wood pestle (called a kok and sak, go to page 75). You will impress all the aunties when you perfect your more delicate pounding technique.

What to Buy at Asian Grocery Store

(NO MORE TRADER JOE'S, HAIYAA . . .)

Western people keep soy sauce, rice vinegar, and sesame oil in their pantry and say they have every ingredient needed to cook anything Asian, haiyaa. There more cooking ingredients from all different regions of Asia than stars in sky. So many, even Asian people sometime get confused on which product to buy. (Asian company love to write label to mess with people. It like their *Squid Game*.) What complicate things further is a lot of time the package instruction is misleading also. And remember what Uncle Roger always say: Don't ever believe any package that say time to cook Asian noodle, always wrong. You gonna overcook it. Only exception is Japanese brand. When I make my Iekei Ramen (page 140), Uncle Roger always follow package instruction for cooking ramen noodle. Japanese people very methodical when they cook, everything precise.

Only read the next few pages if you are Western, especially if your name is Jamie Oliver. Asian people already know what all these ingredient mean. And, VERY important: If no Asian store near where you live, you have NO excuses today for going to bad Western market and buying ingredient that screw up my recipes. (Uncle Roger put my leg down from chair just thinking about it.) In the US, you can buy most ingredient online (pantry, fresh, or frozen) from SayWeee! and they deliver it free to your door. (This shop have dumb name but is super useful.) In the UK, search online for "Asian grocery store." You will find places like Oriental Mart that still think Asian people are rug.

Chilli Pepper, King of Spice!

Chilli pepper go by so many names in different parts of Asia and the West, haiyaa. People even spell it differently. *Chilli* pepper in Asia and most of the rest of the world, *chili* or *chile* pepper in the US and South America. So confusing, haiyaa.

FRESH CHILLIES

No excuses, must have fresh Asian chillies! Uncle Roger sometimes buy a lot of chillies to throw in my freezer so I can make my favorite recipes anytime. And very useful for covering up mistake. Add more chilli, now your dish too hot for anyone to know you screwed up.

Long (pinky-length) red or green Thai chilli: This is the fresh chilli that Uncle Roger use in almost every recipe in my book. "Pinky-length" mean the 2- to 3-inch skinny chilli pepper (called Thai jinda or prik jinda),

what every Southeast Asian and most other Asian market in the West sell in cheap bulk package in produce section. (If package of fifty fresh Thai chilli cost more than a few dollars, you are at wrong market. Expensive Western grocery store trying to rip you off, make you think this a rare, fancy chilli. It grow on side of road in Asia.) These Thai chilli have good, solid heat but are not too hot. If you like things extra spicy, add more to any recipe in my book. (Use feeling!) Green are most common where Uncle Roger live; some come in mix package of red and green. In most recipes, color of chilli does not matter. In others, like my Thai Green Curry Paste (page 166), you MUST use a certain color or your dish will look so bad, everybody think a Westerner made it.

Thai bird's eye chilli: Don't be fooled by the tiny size! Bird's eye chilli pack a punch. Thai name *prik ki nu* mean "mouse poop" because of the shape and size, look very different from longer, skinny Thai jinda chilli. Add one or two bird's eye chillies (three or four if you dare) to any dish, see how you feel on toilet the next day. Uncle Roger approve of adding bird's eye chilli to ANY recipe in my book. Recipes in my book hold back on bird's eye chilli only because it harder to find where I live, Uncle Roger forced to add more pinky-length Thai jinda chilli. Chinese xiao mi la (little rice chilli) is a little less spicy than bird's eye but is good substitute.

Jwala chilli: Any Indian recipe that say "green chilli" like Auntie Shakila's Fuchka (page 77) usually mean jwala, a moderately spicy chilli pepper. (Moderately spicy is fancy way to say mild chilli if you are Asian, extra hot if you are Western.) Jwala are not grown everywhere in the West, so Uncle Roger substitute serrano or green cayenne pepper. Use milder jalapeño ONLY if you are weak and that all you have.

DRIED CHILLIES

Drying fresh chilli in the sun like ancestor bring out its earthy, smoky flavor. (These are NOT smoked like some other dried chillies!) Always soak dried chillies in warm water to soften up before pounding (or chopping) them. Old dried chilli can get a little too dried up, it take a little practice to get them back to pounding.

Small dried red chillies: These are usually 2- to 3-inch red jinda chillies (same as pinky-length Thai chillies) or another variety. Most packages just say "dried chillies," so nobody have any clue what variety it is. Doesn't matter. Chile de árbol, easy to find in the West, also good.

Large mild dried chillies: I add these to my Sambal Tumis (page 64), Thai Red Curry Paste (page 168), and other recipes to give nice deep red color and little extra smokiness. Big guajillo chilli (called mirasol when fresh), about the length of your hand and two finger joints wide, is easy to find in the West, but any other mild dried chilli work. Remember, never use smoked chilli, unless you're making a dish that say to use it, like some Sichuan or Indian food.

Sweeteners

So much Asian food have a little bit of sweetness to balance the explosion of spicy, salty, sour, and other BIG flavors. Most of the time Uncle Roger too cheap to use the sweeteners that ancestor use. I substitute the cheap version that listed in my recipe, like light or dark brown sugar. And even Uncle Roger mum use cheaper white granulated sugar. (Go to page 125 for the BEST recipes in this entire book.) When I feel like something extra special, Uncle Roger pull out these other sugars.

Coconut or palm sugar: Natural coconut or palm sugar have delicious cane flavor. Usually come in little round pieces or chunks, chop up and melt into whatever you cook. *Light* brown sugar (loosely packed!) is Uncle Roger budget substitute.

Gula melaka or jaggery: Mmmm, Uncle Roger love to shave off pieces of these caramel-colored lumps of concentrated sugar with my knife to eat as snack. Malaysian gula melaka make Red Bean Soup (page 221) taste FUIYOH! Gula melaka have a very dark color because coconut palm flower sap boiled down until very thick and rich, then dried. Indian jaggery is similar but can be darker or on the lighter side (some is made from palm sap but other versions use sugar cane). To use, niece and nephew must cook gula melaka or jaggery all the way down until it melts. *Dark* brown sugar is a good substitute in any of my recipes.

Rock sugar: Chinese ancestor take boiled sugarcane syrup and shape it into little lumps that look like translucent rocks, why rock sugar also called sugar ice. Have a mild flavor, good in tea, lighter sauces, and brothy noodle bowl like pho (go to page 156 for Uncle Roger favorite recipe from Niece Tway). Rock sugar take long time to melt, be patient. If you substitute granulated sugar, start with less because rock sugar not as sweet.

__Torch ginger__ Uncle Roger's favorite secret ingredient. I tell you all about on page 49.

Seasonings and Other Staple Ingredients

Uncle Roger have other things in my pantry and refrigerator, but these are the ones I use the most in my recipe.

Soy sauce: When Romans sit around lounging in toga and eating grape, Chinese people were busy inventing one of the greatest sauce of all time. Basic Chinese brand (Lee Kum Kee, Pearl River Bridge) or Japanese brand like Kikkoman is usually all you need. No "lite" or reduced-sodium soy sauce! That like buying low-sugar ketchup. Nobody want tomato sauce on their French fries. If you want to be fancy and splurge, buy a bottle of Jammy Chai First Press Soy Sauce to use when adjust the seasonings after make any dish. Come in pretty ceramic jar company say made from purple sand so can charge even more. Uncle Roger only bring out for special dish when want to impress auntie. But it taste slightly different, have bigger flavor, so use feeling.

White rice vinegar (*unseasoned!*): Western vinegar so harsh, like drinking acid. Rice vinegar can be subtle or intense, so many different kind: white, black, red, barely aged, or sealed up in ceramic jar for years. The cheap kind at any Asian (and Western) grocery store, like Marukan, is what Uncle Roger use every day and in most of my recipes.

Shaoxing rice wine: This rice wine is FUIYOH! Made from fermented glutinous rice, yeast, and water. It give stir-fry, marinades, and even my Takeout-Style Egg Rolls (page 109) extra depth of flavor. A little splash (not too much) make people think you real Chinese chef. Cheap bottle of Liang brand (wine is spelled *shao hsing* on label) last Uncle Roger for months.

Coconut milk: Full-fat coconut milk only! All other taste like water. For recipes that use coconut cream, get a good, really THICK coconut cream. Read label, should have almost no water. In Malaysia we call this santan; go to page 135 if you don't know what it is.

Belacan: This is Southeast Asian shrimp paste. It come in little blocks of hard paste. Shrimp & 6A brand in yellow package is most common in the West, it will still be good in your fridge when you die. Slice off little nub, then you have to toast it to release the flavor and aroma. Belacan is how you get best seat on subway. Open little container of my Sambal Belacan (page 66) from your lunch tote. Everybody move out of the way.

Block tamarind: SEEDLESS Indian or Thai slab (or block) tamarind is the type of tamarind Uncle Roger use for all recipes in my book. (Thai tamarind concentrate that come in jar is very different, cooked down to a thick, sticky, molasses texture.) Niece and nephew always must soften block tamarind in hot water for a few minutes, smash tamarind and water together with fingers. Then make sure get out any last bits of seed (seedless block still have a few coarse bits). If you really want, you can push the softened tamarind through a strainer with bigger mesh holes, the kind people use to wash lettuce or other vegetable. (No fine-mesh sieve! Too much work and you get very little paste.*) Always easier to just pick out any coarse bits of seed or skin with your fingers, and you get a bigger amount of usable paste. (Auntie Shakila's Tamarind Pani on page 81 is the exception. Good to use a fancy fine-mesh sieve. *Pani* mean "water," not supposed to be lumpy.) Rani, King, and Happy Panda are all good brands of seedless tamarind. Wrap up the leftover block of tamarind to keep in refrigerator for months.

Makrut lime (Thai name is *magrood*, *kaffir* is old English name): Peel have bumpy, dark skin, give things like Thai curry paste (pages 164 to 169) its bright flavor, so much better than Western lime. If no Thai lime where you live, Western lime peel OK. Makrut lime leaf is used in actual curry (pages 171 to 181) and other dishes. It have BIG citrusy aroma and little more subtle flavor than peel. No good substitute for makrut lime leaf, look for it fresh (best), frozen (OK), or dried at Asian market. If dried only option, don't chop up if recipe say to, leave whole.

Fine table salt: Why so many Westerners waste their money on fancy salt? Sea salt (so many sizes and types, haiyaa), kosher salt, fleur de sel. (*Fleur* sound like a flower, not something Uncle Roger want to eat.) Uncle Roger use cheap table salt, kind that come in blue box with girl holding umbrella that can get at every grocery store. Cheap and delicious, and have super-fine granules, so my food never underseasoned. Umbrella brand (Morton) makes their famous table salt with or without iodine today. (You choose, but ancestor not afraid of a little iodized table salt.) If use another salt that have larger granules when you make my recipe, need to increase the salt. If your food have no flavor, that your fault.

---

*Uncle Roger make mistake one time, buy regular (not seedless) block tamarind. It so full of seed (and skin), I have to smash the softened pulp through a fine mesh sieve for 15 minute and have only a tiny bit of paste to use, haiyaa.

MSG, King of Flavor (FUIYOH!)

MSG in category all by itself. Nothing compare to the flavor. Uncle Roger always buy cheap bag of Aji-No-Moto, but it doesn't matter what brand you get. MSG all taste the same. Only thing that matter is how much you use.

Other Pantry Ingredients

OK, Uncle Roger hand hurt from so much typing, haiyaa. Just flip to the pages listed for the rest of these other ingredients if you don't know what type to buy.

Black salt (kala namak): page 87

Chana dal (split chickpeas): page 80

Char siu *(Everybody know what this is, even Western people, haiyaa. But Uncle Roger tell you why you don't ever want to make it. Other cookbook lie to you, say you can make good version at home.)*: **page 192**

Chinese doubanjiang (fermented broad bean with chilli): page 99

Cilantro (coriander) root: page 167

Dried hawthorn berries: page 197

Fermented black crab paste *(Nam pu is Lao ingredient, Uncle Roger put in book so don't get canceled again by Laos.)*: **page 75**

Fermented fish sauce *(stinky but delicious, for authentic Lao food)*: **page 75**

Fermented red bean curd: page 131

Kecap manis: page 86

Keropok (fish or shrimp crackers): page 128

Lap cheong (Chinese sausage): page 40

Malaysian meat curry powder *(Uncle Roger mum use this as her secret weapon!)*: **page 135**

Pandan leaves: page 186

Pressed tofu: page 84

Sago pearls *(This ingredient even confuse Asian people.)*: **page 220**

Santan *(extra-thick coconut cream, FUIYOH!)*: **page 135**

Shah jeera (black cumin): page 212

Torch ginger flower *(Uncle Roger favorite ingredient of all time!)*: **page 49**

XO sauce: page 45

NutriAsia
AJINOMOTO
AJI-NO-MOTO
味の素
UMAMI SEASONING
SINCE 1909
MONOSODIUM GLUTAMATE
NET WT 16 OZ (1 LB) 454g
TRADITIONALLY BREWED
ALL-PURPOSE
SEASONING
KIKKOMAN
NO PRESERVATIVES ADDED
TRADITIONALLY BREWED
Soy Sauce
1.25 QT (1.2 L)
良
特
選
紹兴料酒

How to Make Rice

HAIYAA, WHY DOES UNCLE ROGER EVEN HAVE TO PUT THIS CHAPTER IN MY BOOK?

Types of Rice

There are only two type of rice: jasmine, and all other rice.*

There are exceptions, yes, like sticky rice, sushi rice, and fluffy basmati rice, but jasmine is Uncle Roger favorite. When you steam it, make whole house smell good, and perfect for fry rice (see page 37) and in most other rice dish. (Calrose is also good, but expensive. Spend your money on rice cooker.) And white rice matters! Brown rice is healthy, sure, but it taste like dirt.

Uncle Roger Steam Rice Rules

1. **How many times do I have to say ALWAYS use a rice cooker?†**
   Uncle Roger refuse to write down a recipe for a stovetop method to cook rice. World War II is over, use technology. You have electricity, a refrigerator, stove, oven, toaster. Just go buy a rice cooker. Uncle Roger like baby elephant brand Zojirushi. It sing lullaby to me when rice is done. But even cheap rice cooker is better than none. Don't give me that, "Oh but rice cooker is single-purpose appliance, I don't have space in my kitchen for that." Trust Uncle Roger—once you get rice cooker, you will use it every day, and you actually save space because now you don't need to use one of your burner on your stove for rice. Besides, coffee machine also single-purpose, but you don't see anyone complaining that their home too small for that, haiyaa.

*Western people, leave rice to Asian farmer! Western grocery store rice stale with hard texture and have no smell. All life drained out of it. They come in the tiniest packet. Who eating this little Splenda packet of rice? Is your whole family just baby bird? Is the baby bird on diet? Or even worse, sometime they ask you to microwave, haiyaa. Go to Asian market, buy 25-pound bag *jasmine* rice. Drag to car like you doing CrossFit.

†Indian dish like biryani (see page 208) is one exception. Basmati rice is only partly cooked on the stovetop because it finishes cooking in the oven. Rice cooker would make it mushy. Another is Lao sticky rice. Cook in bamboo steamer basket to get nice sticky texture. But rice cooker still work!

2. **Measure rice, then rinse. Don't soak.***

   Wash your rice! Good for rice and your mental health. Just you and rice, so peaceful, don't need therapy. Rinse until water runs clear. Drain. Uncle Roger like to wash my rice three time for good luck.

3. **Use rice cooker to measure correct amount of water.**

   The only thing two Asian people will agree on at family dinner table is how much water to use in rice cooker. Answer is whatever the rice cooker bowl say. This is what the water fill lines are for. Auntie and uncle who still live ancestor lifestyle will insist everybody do finger test with index finger. OK, OK, that work. One exception: Finger test rule does not apply to Yao Ming. His hand too big. If he use his finger to do finger test, you gonna end up with congee.

4. **Steamed rice have NO seasonings!†**

   Just rinsed rice and correct amount of water. Fine, if you want you can add pinch of salt, but trust me, it not needed. The rice gonna be paired with delicious dishes. Don't need to flavor rice, let it be blank canvas.

5. **Hit play button on rice cooker. Walk away.**

   Uncle Roger daydream about my favorite auntie. Open my eyes, rice is ready.

6. **Always save leftover steam rice!**

   Let rice cool and cover. (Never leave cooked rice naked, dry out too much. Cover with plastic, kitchen towel, whatever you have.) Put in refrigerator one, two, or three days. Now you can make one of Uncle Roger's favorite styles of fry rice in next chapter (see page 37). Leave rice longer than three day and it dry out too much. Now perfect for my favorite Crispy Fried Rice Bits (page 58).

*Some Indian aunties like to soak basmati rice, that OK. (Some don't.) Japanese sushi rice and sticky Thai or Lao rice for green papaya salad (get my salad recipes on pages 67 and 73) are always soaked because they are more glutinous. Still rinse first!

†Seasoning allowed ONLY if make flavored rice like Coconut Rice (page 186) or need to salt rice for Auntie Shakila's Biryani (page 208). Mmmm, both so good.

ZOJIRUSHI
COOK
KEEP WARM

ZOJIRUSHI
COOK
KEEP
WARM

Good Mor

Good

FRY RICE

(FUIYOH!)

UNCLE ROGER CAN WRITE WHOLE
BOOK ON JUST FRY RICE BUT ONLY HAVE ROOM
FOR A FEW OF MY FAVORITE.

UNCLE ROGER'S EGG FRY RICE

(The recipe that started it all)

SERVES 1

(Uncle Roger could eat this whole thing as appetizer but watching my figure.)

Ah, the classic egg fry rice, the dish that turn Uncle Roger into D-list Internet celebrity. Uncle Roger always say, egg fry rice only three ingredient: egg, fry, and rice. This recipe is my perfected version with more detail so everybody can make Uncle Roger favorite fry rice at home. (FUIYOH!) Don't even think about starting until you have all your ingredient prepped and in separate dishes. Unless you are auntie or uncle level at making fry rice, even cracking the egg can slow you down. But remember: Egg fry rice is SO simple. You can do this. Make Uncle Roger proud.

Neutral oil, for seasoning the wok

Finely ground white pepper

MSG, King of Flavor

About 1 tablespoon Pork Lard *(page 42; Vegetable oil OK ONLY if that all you have in the house, haiyaa.)*

1 finger-length (4- to 5-inch) piece lap cheong (Chinese sausage, *read Uncle Roger note!)***, thinly sliced** *(Thin but not razor thin. You want to see the sausage but not gnaw on it.)*

2 tablespoons finely chopped shallots *(That mean two spoonful, use feeling!)*

3 to 4 garlic cloves, finely chopped

1 egg *(Add 1 egg yolk for extra flavor and cholesterol, FUIYOH!)*

1 Asian-size bowl (about 1 cup) day-old rice, broken up with your fingers *(day or two old, sat in fridge)*

About 1½ tablespoons soy sauce

About 1 tablespoon sesame oil

2 scallions, sliced *(Green part of spring only only!)*

1 to 2 long (pinky-length) red or green Thai chillies or bird's eye chillies, sliced

Optional: 1 or more Fry Rice Additions *(Once you master egg fry rice, it is the perfect fry rice to change up with my special additions. Uncle Roger tell you how to add them after recipe.)*

Have all of your ingredients prepped and ready in separate dishes. *(Did you read entire recipe? Reading while you cook take up too much time, haiyaa. Put spatula down and read the whole recipe now.)*

Heat a wok over high heat until hot. Add about 2 tablespoons neutral oil and tilt the wok to coat the surface. Heat the oil for a minute or two, then dump it out. *(Seasoning wok is very important first step!)* Reheat the wok, add the pork lard and heat again until the fat starts to smoke. *(No cheating! Turn up stove all the way or won't get wok hei.)*

Recipe continues

Reduce the heat to medium. *(Not what fry rice expert do, but this is so home cook don't burn the ingredient.)* Add the Chinese sausage, shallots, and garlic and stir-fry a few seconds. *(Fry sausage and aromatics just a few seconds, not too long.)* Add the egg and break it up with the wok turner only until very loosely set. *(Bang, bang, bang on the bottom of the wok. If fry eggs more than a few seconds, they overcook.)*

(Crank back up the heat from now on or you won't get wok hei, haiyaa.) Add the rice and spread it out with the wok turner so it doesn't clump together. Add the soy sauce and sesame oil and toss and stir until the rice darkens from the soy sauce. *(Sometimes this takes a while, depends on your heat. If ingredient start to burn, just move wok off the burner for a few second, buy yourself a little time. Take a breath. Fry rice will be OK.)*

Sprinkle 2 to 3 pinches of white pepper and 1 BIG pinch of MSG all over the rice. *(Relationship is like egg fry rice. Sometime you think everything going well, but if you forget to put MSG in there, it all fall apart.)* Toss and stir a few more times and adjust the seasoning with soy sauce, sesame oil, or MSG. *(Taste! You are the fry rice chef.)*

Scatter the scallions and chillies over the rice and keep tossing and stirring until no clumps of rice remain. *(You know fry rice ready when individual grains of rice jumping up. Very exciting when it happen.)* Take the wok off the heat. *(This really just an excuse to taste your fry rice creation one more time.)*

Scrape the fried rice onto a plate. *(What are you waiting for? Need to eat fry rice immediately. Don't leave it waiting. If your family want some, they can wait. Make another portion when you finish.)*

× HAIYAA . . .

GOOD fry rice must be fried in Pork Lard (page 42). Make your own or buy it. No excuses.

DO NOT overcrowd your wok. If you cooking at home, your stove probably not super high power, so you should only cook one portion at a time. If you want to make 2 portion of egg fry rice, then repeat process twice. Don't try to put 2 portion of rice in wok, you not gonna be able to cook properly.

LAP CHEONG (CHINESE SAUSAGE)

This the ONLY option for egg fry rice. Very distinct flavor, seasoned with soy sauce, sugar, and rice wine, then dried and smoked. Don't even think about Western sausage for substitute! If no Asian market nearby, please, please buy online, or borrow from your nearest Chinese neighbor. In Asia, you can buy it fresh, come in all different sizes. In the West, it come in convenient vacuum-sealed bag so it OK to keep in pantry. Only need to refrigerate when open.

Weejios

Uncle Roger Disgusted by this Egg Fried Rice Video (BBC Food) *This the weejio that started it all. Uncle Roger remember the first time I saw this weejio—I in shock, disgust, anger, all the emotion.*

Uncle Roger Make Egg Fried Rice (@the_modernchef)

Uncle Roger Review Biggest Fried Rice Myth (@MadewithLau)

Uncle Roger Amazed by Perfect Egg Fried Rice (@ChefWang)

Fry Rice Additions

These are the ONLY Uncle Roger–approved changes to my fry rice recipe. Go read those recipes in Up Your Fry Rice Game (page 53) first. Uncle Roger repeat myself here to make sure Western people don't mess anything up.

Uncle Roger's Crispy Fried Egg (page 54): Make the fried rice as instructed. *(Uncle Roger like double egg: Egg in fry rice and still put this on top.)* In a separate skillet or wok, fry the crispy egg at the same time you make the fried rice. *(Or immediately after you fry your rice. Fry rice will wait for you.)* Serve the fried egg on top of the fried rice.

Crispy Fried Rice Bits (page 58): *(This one is Uncle Roger favorite add-on. Sure to impress all your friend.)* Fry a small handful (about 5 tablespoons) of dried rice bits. *(Fry your rice bits in hot oil BEFORE you start your fry rice, go read that technique. Want them nice and crunchy.)* When the fried rice is ready to serve, turn off the heat. Add about three-quarters of the rice bits to the wok and toss and stir to combine it with the fried rice. *(Remember, must be at very end or rice bits get soggy, lose nice crunchy texture.)* Scrape the fried rice onto a plate and scatter the remaining rice bits on top. *(FUIYOH!)*

THE Egg Floss (page 57): Omit the egg in the fried rice recipe. *(Still add your cooked egg floss to the hot wok after you fry the sausage and aromatics.)* Toss and stir until the egg strands just begin to lightly brown, then add the rice and other ingredients as instructed.

Have all of your ingredients prepped and ready in separate dishes. *(If you are adding my crispy fried rice bits, fry those up first, put on plate. Go read that recipe, it tell you how. Now your wok is seasoned, ready to go. FUIYOH!)*

Heat a wok over high heat until hot. Add about 2 tablespoons neutral oil and tilt the wok to coat the surface. Heat the oil for a minute or two, then dump it out.

Reheat the wok until smoking, add the pork lard, and heat again. *(Fat should start to smoke, stove cranked all the way up!)*

Reduce the heat to medium. *(Not what expert do, but this for fry rice first-timers. So don't burn the ingredient.)* Add the Chinese sausage, shallots, and garlic and stir-fry a few seconds. *(Fry sausage and aromatics quickly to release flavor.)* Add the egg and break it up with your wok turner only until very loosely set; it shouldn't fully solidify. *(Bang, bang, bang on the bottom of the wok. Don't overcook egg! Should not be fully cooked.)*

(Turn heat back to high from now on so get wok hei.) Add the rice and spread it out with your wok turner so it doesn't clump together. Add the XO sauce, toss and stir a few times to integrate the sauce, then add the soy sauce and sesame oil and toss again. Add the oyster mushrooms *(if using)* and toss and stir until the rice darkens from the sauces and the mushrooms soften. *(Same thing apply as when make egg fry rice. Sometimes this stage take a while, depend on how good you are at maintaining the heat. If ingredient start to burn, just move the wok off the burner for a few seconds, buy yourself a little time.)*

Sprinkle 2 to 3 pinches of white pepper and 1 BIG pinch of MSG all over the rice. Toss and stir a few more times. Adjust the seasonings with soy sauce, sesame oil, or MSG.

Scatter the long beans, scallions, and chillies over the rice and keep tossing and stirring until no clumps of rice remain. *(Almost there! Wait for individual grains of rice to start jumping up.)* Take the wok off the heat. *(Did you fry up some crispy fry rice bits? Now is the time to fold about three-quarters into your fry rice. Have to do at the last minute so they stay crispy.)*

Scrape the fried rice onto a plate and scatter the remaining crispy fried rice bits over the fried rice and the strips of scallion greens, if using. *(Mmmm, Uncle Roger want some XO fry rice right now.)*

✕ HAIYAA . . .

Only Jamie Oliver use sausage other than lap cheong (see page 40). No substitute! Don't you dare use European 'nduja.

And don't overcrowd your wok and try to cook more than one portion of fry rice at a time, haiyaa. Go read page 40!

✓ FUIYOH!

Some cook use char siu in XO fry rice (OK, OK), but Uncle Roger like lap cheong. Always have in my pantry and Chinese sausage not sweet like char siu, balance fry rice flavor better.

Little bit of crunchy long bean give nice texture contrast to rice (long bean perfect because have no flavor). If Uncle Roger have fresh oyster mushroom, throw in skillet for extra umami and good mouthfeel. Crispy fried rice bits take my XO fry rice over the top!

XO SAUCE

Lee Kum Kee XO Sauce with black and gold label is what Uncle Roger have in my refrigerator. Same company make a cheaper version in red jar called Seafood XO Sauce to make people think it just as fancy. Not as good, have less premium seafood.

UNCLE ROGER'S SPECIAL FRY RICE

(Special mean delicious.)

SERVES 1

Jamie Oliver could never handle this fry rice. It too delicious. Flavor explode on your tongue. So easy to make: Add a little of my favorite sambal (Uncle Roger's Sambal Belacan, see page 66) and the BEST Southeast Asian ingredient, torch ginger, to my Egg Fry Rice (page 38), now it extra special. We serve a variation of this at my restaurant, FUIYOH! It's Uncle Roger.

Neutral oil, for seasoning the wok

Finely ground white pepper

MSG, King of Flavor

About 2½ tablespoons finely chopped fresh torch ginger flower *(Chop pink part only. No substitute! If don't have any, Uncle Roger feel sorry for you.)*

About 1½ tablespoons Sambal Belacan (page 66), drained of excess liquid

About 1 tablespoon Pork Lard (page 42; *haiyaa, vegetable oil OK only if that all you have.)*

1 finger-length (4- to 5-inch) piece lap cheong (Chinese sausage; see page 40), thinly sliced *(Uncle Roger ONLY add sausage if I have no torch ginger!)*

About 2 tablespoons finely chopped shallots

3 to 4 garlic cloves, finely chopped

1 egg *(Add 1 egg yolk for extra flavor and cholesterol, we all going to die anyway.)*

1 Asian-size bowl (about 1 cup) day-old rice, broken up with your fingers *(day or two old, sat in fridge)*

About 1 tablespoon soy sauce

About 1 tablespoon sesame oil

2 scallions, sliced *(Remember, green onion is garnish! Green part only.)*

TO SERVE

About ½ Western lime *(Sliced like Thai auntie; go to page 70 if you Western and don't know how.)*

Optional *(but FUIYOH!)*: **A small handful (about 5 tablespoons) of Crispy Fried Rice Bits (page 58)**

Have all of your ingredients prepped and ready in separate dishes. Set aside 2 tablespoons of torch ginger and 1 tablespoon of sambal belacan for stir-frying. *(Don't mix together, haiyaa. Keep in separate little dish!)* Save the remaining torch ginger and sambal for serving.

Heat a wok over high heat until hot. Add about 2 tablespoons neutral oil and tilt the wok to coat the surface. Heat the oil for a minute or two, then dump it out. *(Why does Uncle Roger have to keep telling you to season wok, haiyaa. Remember, if frying my crispy fried rice bits, do it now.)*

Reheat the wok until smoking, add the pork lard and heat again. *(Wait until fat start to smoke, how you know it ready.)* Add the Chinese sausage *(only if missing torch ginger . . .)*, shallots, and garlic and stir-fry a few seconds. *(Fry sausage and aromatics just a few seconds only, to release flavor.)*

Recipe continues

Reduce the heat to medium. *(Remember, reducing heat is not authentic. This is so fry rice first-timers don't burn the ingredient.)* Add the egg and break it up with your wok turner only until very loosely set; it shouldn't fully solidify. *(Bang, bang, bang on the bottom of the wok.)*

(Remember, turn heat back to high now so get wok hei.) Add the rice and spread it out with your wok turner so it doesn't clump together. Add the 2 tablespoons torch ginger, 1 tablespoon sambal balacan, soy sauce, and sesame oil and toss and stir until the rice darkens from the soy sauce. *(Stay focused! If get distracted, move the wok off the burner for a few seconds to keep garlic from burning.)*

Sprinkle 2 or 3 pinches of white pepper and 1 BIG pinch of MSG all over the rice. Toss and stir a few more times. Scatter the scallions and chillies over the rice and keep tossing and stirring until no clumps of rice remain. *(Wait until individual grains of rice to start jumping up. Enjoy the smell of the torch ginger, FUIYOH!)*

When the fried rice is ready, add the remaining ½ tablespoon sambal balacan and toss and stir just to fully incorporate. Take the wok off the heat and add a generous squeeze of lime juice. Adjust the seasonings with soy sauce, sesame oil, or MSG. *(No more lime now, going to serve fry rice with lime slices. And did you fry up some crispy fried rice bits? Now is the time to fold about three-quarters of them into your fry rice. Have to do at the last minute so they stay crispy.)*

Scrape the fried rice onto a plate. Scatter the remaining ½ tablespoon torch ginger and crispy fried rice bits on top, if using.

Serve the fried rice with the remaining sliced lime. *(Squeeze lime over fry rice right before eat it. Nice bright, fresh flavor.)*

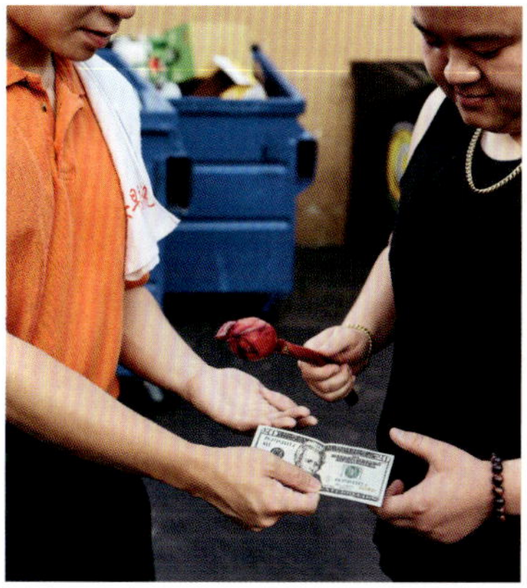

× HAIYAA . . .

One last time, lap cheong is ONLY sausage that is acceptable in fry rice! And don't need it if have torch ginger. We want torch ginger to SHINE.

Sambal belacan is NOT the same as the sambal oelek that is at every Western grocery store. Just go make some—it will be your new favorite sambal.

Only cook one portion of fry rice at a time (see page 40 with my egg fry rice) or you will screw it up!

TORCH GINGER FLOWER

(also called wild ginger bud): Every time Uncle Roger go to Asia, first thing I do is go to my restaurant and order my special fry rice with sambal and torch ginger flower. Such a pretty pink flower, taste NOTHING like common ginger. It more floral, not spicy. It give fry rice and anything else it touches a delicious flavor and aroma and nice slightly pink color. Some American auntie and uncle may be able to get torch ginger in humid places like Florida or Hawaii. (It can grow there, so use as a flower for leis. Only reason to go on such expensive vacation.) Or go to Malaysia and bring some back in suitcase, grow in your greenhouse. (Asian people ignore airport customs.) For cookbook, Uncle Roger have to import this flower from Ecuador, $25 per flower, haiyaa. Niece and nephew, please start growing torch ginger flower in your backyard and sell to me cheaper!

KIMCHI FRY RICE

(Kimchi Bokkeumbap)

SERVES 1 OR 2

Two facts: First, not everybody who is Asian like kimchi like Western people—and Auntie Esther—think. (Uncle Roger like GOOD kimchi. But kimchi have a unique flavor and can sometime get a little too sour . . . just like Uncle Roger favorite Korean auntie.) Second, not every Asian culture makes good fry rice. (Why do Korean people only make fry rice to use up old kimchi that been sitting in refrigerator for six month? Haiyaa, don't do that to your fry rice.)

Uncle Roger teach every niece and nephew how to make perfect kimchi fry rice. Not even going to give you an ingredient list. Don't need it. Just go watch my weejio with Auntie Maangchi when she make her shrimp and scallop kimchi fry rice. Auntie Maangchi is very good Korean cook, and so friendly. Always waving at Uncle Roger. Then go watch weejio when Auntie Esther cook her bacon kimchi fried rice for Nephew Nigel. Mix their two recipe together, now you can make very good kimchi fry rice.

STEP 1

Make Uncle Roger's Spicy Kimchi (page 89). It take at least 3 to 4 weeks to ferment enough for kimchi fry rice, want it more on sour side, not fresh. Plenty of time to make other recipes in book, forget about kimchi fry rice. Now you don't need to make it. *(Uncle Roger going to get canceled by another country.)*

STEP 2

Still want to make kimchi fry rice? OK, OK, Uncle Roger only have a few tiny words of advice for Auntie Maangchi. Uncle Roger remind you most important part of my weejio:

- **Shrimp is good. Don't need scallop. Fried rice not supposed to bankrupt niece and nephew.**
- **Auntie Maangchi wash chopping board after chopping kimchi. That show she real Korean auntie. Kimchi so stinky, must wash cutting board.** *(Kimchi smell ruin every food that touch cutting board for whole month. Chicken only give family salmonella, much less annoying.)*
- **Scallion, good. Fish sauce, nice. Portable gas stove, FUIYOH! Uncle Roger LOVE Auntie Maangchi.**
- **Vegetable oil, good. Auntie Maangchi know what she doing.**
- **Wait, what? Nooooo. No water goes in fry rice! Kimchi brine only.** *(Not too much or fry rice will be wet.)*
- **And why Auntie Maangchi cook fry rice in a pan, cover with lid? That paella. Must use wok for WOK HEI! Auntie Maangchi so close, then her Korean come out.** *(That OK. She not from China, where fry rice invented, so Uncle Roger forgive her and all Korean people. Western people have no excuse for ruining fry rice.)*

STEP 3

Now Uncle Roger watch Auntie Esther weejio. She make kimchi fry rice right before Uncle Roger make her his special noodle. (Auntie Esther love spicy Malaysian noodle.) Auntie Esther have no excuses because she fancy New York chef.

- Fry bacon, OK, good. Pork fat make everything better. But why not using Pork Lard (page 42)? Bacon fat have too much flavor.
- How Auntie Esther Asian chef, and only have cast-iron skillet? Hmmm.
- Wait, what? Auntie Esther also like wet kimchi fry rice?
- OK, she use good quality kimchi, nice. *(Auntie Esther probably use Uncle Roger recipe.)*
- Scallions, good. Maybe go in pan a little early.
- Auntie Esther also use gochujang, haiyaa. What? Don't need, already in kimchi. Was looking so good, too.
- OK, now she make her fry rice extra spicy with scorpion peppers. Auntie Esther know how Uncle Roger like it.
- Day-old rice, good. Fish sauce, correct. Nice crispy bottom on rice.
- Fried egg, pretty good. Some producer fry egg ahead for Auntie Esther, why only deserve a "pretty good." Uncle Roger's Crispy Fried Egg (page 54) so much better.
- Seaweed garnish, also good, very Korean.
- Nephew Nigel tasting now. Looks like he like it. Auntie Esther can't handle hot pepper, Uncle Roger can't handle cold shoulder.
- Haiyaa, Uncle Roger give up. Fly all the way to Malaysia to go to my own restaurant. Order any other fry rice.

Weejios

Uncle Roger Review Maangchi Kimchi Fried Rice (with @Maangchi)

Uncle Roger Cooks Spicy Malaysian Noodles for Auntie Esther (with @choibites)

UP YOUR FRY RICE GAME

When Uncle Roger have time, I make something special for my fry rice. I love a classic *Asian* fried egg (see page 54) on top of my rice with nice, crispy browned edges. When I have enough patience, I sometime make my version of Uncle Wang Gang's egg floss (page 57) to replace the egg in the fry rice. But my all-time favorite thing is my crispy little puffs of deep-fry rice grains (see Crispy Fried Rice Bits, page 58). Stir into ANY fry rice at the end, when take wok off stove, for a tiny pop of crunch and toasty flavor. FUIYOH!

UNCLE ROGER'S CRISPY FRIED EGG

MAKES 1 FRIED EGG

This not your typical fried egg at the Holiday Inn breakfast buffet. This is NOT white, flavorless sunny side up egg. Asian people like egg with color. A perfect fry egg has crispy, golden-brown edges because it is *fried*. And the yolk rehydrate the rice, give it fatty, creamy texture. It take fry rice to the next level or make a plain bowl of steam rice a meal. Fry up my egg anytime you need a delicious, creamy protein. (Sorry, children.)

Neutral oil, for deep-frying

1 egg

Line a plate with a paper towel. Fill a wok with 1 finger joint (about 1 inch) oil. *(Use feeling! When add egg to wok later, egg should be partly submerged in oil so edges get crispy, but not so much oil that the yolk will fry up too fast.)* Heat the oil until very hot; if the oil smokes, turn down the heat and let it cool slightly. *(Hot but not too hot or will cook egg too fast.)*

Crack the egg directly over the oil; it should sizzle and pop vigorously. With a wok turner, quickly scoop up and splash the hot oil over the whites closest to the edges; avoid the whites closest to the yolk. *(Basting whites at edges of egg help them get browned and crispy. Want whites at edges to get right color but don't want to cook yolk yet.)* When the whites are nicely browned, coat the yolk with hot oil just until barely set. *(Want nice runny middle.)*

(Now take egg out, put on paper towel to drain excess oil. Ready to slide that egg on top of anything, especially fry rice!)

✔ FUIYOH!

When Uncle Roger spend 24 hours in Bangkok with Mark Wiens, I get to watch Chef Gigg at Mark Wiens's restaurant, Phed Mark, make an EXTRA crispy fry duck egg. It have that rich, brown Asian color all over. Watch weejio if you want to try to make it. It not as easy as it look, Uncle Roger try before. Good luck.

Weejio

Uncle Roger Almost Died: 24 Hours in Thailand (with @MarkWiens)

Weejio

Uncle Roger Love Insane Egg Fried Rice Technique (with @ChefWang and @AdamLiaw)

THE EGG FLOSS

ENOUGH FOR 1 SERVING OF FRIED RICE *(Easiest to make a lot of egg floss at one time. Might as well eat whole thing yourself. Going to die someday.)*

Nobody ever going to make egg floss as good as Uncle Wang Gang, but this recipe get close enough. Not as hard as it looks. All the badass aunties make egg floss, even Uncle Roger mum. (FUIYOH!)

Neutral oil, for deep-frying

3 eggs *(This mean whatever egg you have. Asian people don't care what size your egg.)*

Set a fine-mesh sieve over a measuring cup. *(Uncle Wang put egg in bowl. For Uncle Roger, it easier to pour a very thin stream of egg out of cup with a little pour spout. Uncle Wang also use very fine mesh strainer. That work best, but whatever you have OK, you get a little less smooth floss.)* **Crack the eggs into the sieve and lightly whisk with chopsticks.** *(Not too much whisking or get air into egg! Uncle Roger not teaching you to make a soufflé, haiyaa.)* **Press the eggs through the sieve with your fingers.** *(Take a very long time if have fine sieve.)*

Fill a wok with 1 finger joint (about 1 inch) oil and heat over medium heat just until hot. *(Not too hot! Egg floss like it gentle. Around 200°F/95°C is perfect, but oil can be a little hotter. Don't need thermometer. If egg puff up, get angry at you when add a tiny bit to wok, temperature too hot.)*

Line a plate with paper towels and put it near the stove. With a wok turner or chopsticks, constantly stir the oil in a wide circle around the edges of the wok. *(Want nice movement, constant stirring, but not too fast or will break up egg strands. See? Harder than it sounds to make egg floss.)* **Keep stirring while you slowly pour about one-third of the eggs into the wok in a very thin stream.** *(Haiyaa, did your eggs puff up? Stop and scoop out egg puffs. Turn off heat for a minute, let cool a little, start again.)* **As the strands of egg form, keep gently stirring in a wide circle.** *(Accept now that you are not Uncle Wang. Floss will not be perfect. You will get some clumps of egg in strands.)* **Cook the egg strands just until set, about 15 seconds.** *(Egg will get brown color when cook again in fry rice.)* **Gently scoop out the strands with chopsticks and a wok turner or a spider.** *(Two utensils help get up all strands.)* **Transfer the eggs to the paper towels and pat the top of the strands with a paper towel to soak up some of the excess oil.**

(Now ready to add egg floss to your fry rice! Uncle Roger already tell you how in my egg fry rice recipe, but have to repeat myself in cookbook.)

TO ADD THE EGG FLOSS TO FRIED RICE

Omit the egg in Uncle Roger's Egg Fried Rice (page 38) recipe. *(Add your egg floss to the hot wok AFTER frying the sausage and aromatics.)* Toss and stir until the egg strands just begin to lightly brown, then add the rice and other ingredients as instructed.

× HAIYAA . . .

Pushing yolk through sieve take patience of a Chinese chef. If lazy, whisk egg with a chopstick. Floss will have bits of egg white instead of uniform yellow color but will taste the same.

CRISPY FRIED RICE BITS

MAKES ABOUT 1½ CUPS, ENOUGH FOR 4 OR 5 SERVINGS OF FRIED RICE

This a crowd favorite at Uncle Roger restaurant. It put some unexpected crunch in your fry rice, add some interesting texture, gonna delight your guest. And a good way to use up old rice. When you leave leftover rice in fridge too long, it gonna dry out too much like Uncle Roger ex-wife. Make these crispy little puffs of deep-fried rice bits. Keep in sealed bag in pantry for a whole month. Now have extra-special fry rice whenever you want it.

About 2 cups OLD cooked rice *(4, 5, 6 day old perfect, younger 1 or 2 day old cooked rice also OK)*

Neutral oil, for deep-frying

Break apart the rice and spread it out in a single layer on a baking sheet. *(Give rice grains plenty of room so they dry out. Best to use baking sheet with rim so you don't spill rice all over oven when you pull out pan.)* Leave the rice at room temperature for a few hours to dry out. *(Exact time doesn't matter. Just let rice get some air.)*

Preheat the oven to 300°F (150°C).

Bake the rice for 15 minutes. Take the baking sheet out of the oven and redistribute the rice so the driest grains are toward the center of the pan; break up any larger clumps. Bake for another 15 minutes, turn the oven off, and let the rice cool in the oven for about 1 hour. The grains should be very dry. *(If not dry, your rice probably too wet when you cook it. That OK. Turn oven back on, bake for another 5 to 10 minutes, check again.)*

Store the dried rice at room temperature for 1 month or longer. *(Keep in tightly sealed bag or container with a little piece of paper towel so rice bits stay crispy.)*

To fry the rice bits: Start with a handful (about 5 tablespoons) of the dried rice per serving. *(You can fry rice bits right before you start to cook your fry rice. Or if having a fry rice party, fry these up an hour or two ahead, as long as your kitchen isn't too humid. Don't want soggy rice bits, haiyaa. Cook as much as you want at one time. Rice bits are good on everything, not just fry rice, you will eat them all! Just make sure you have enough oil to deep-fry.)* Line a plate with paper towels.

After seasoning your wok, add enough oil to deep-fry the rice bits and heat until moderately hot. *(Hot but not smoking.)* Add the dried rice. *(Are rice bits covered in oil? Good job.)* Deep-fry the rice, stirring occasionally and breaking up any large clumps, until light golden brown, 2 to 3 minutes. *(Light brown color give nice flavor. Too brown and rice will taste bitter.)* Transfer the rice bits to the plate to drain.

Set the crispy fried rice bits aside until ready to use or for up to 2 to 3 hours in a dry location. *(If your house is humid, cold oven is a good place.)* Stir the crispy fried rice bits into or sprinkle them on top of any dish right before serving to keep them crunchy. *(Now go to page 38 and make Uncle Roger's Egg Fry Rice with your crispy rice bits!)*

✔ FUIYOH!

Throw sliced Thai chillies (sliced garlic good, too) into wok when rice bits almost ready, the last 30 second. Season with salt. Mmmm . . . delicious, high-fat fry rice snack!

媽媽 清湯
INSTANT RICE VERMICELLI CLEAR SOUP
MAMA
SIN QUA
Turmeric
LONGBEAN
CELERY
Good Mornin
DAIKON

THE ONLY VEGETABLE UNCLE ROGER EAT

MOST VEGETABLE TASTE LIKE SAD. THE VEGETABLE IN THIS CHAPTER ARE THE ONLY ONES UNCLE ROGER EAT BECAUSE THEY HAVE BIG FLAVOR. YES, SAMBAL AND PEANUT COUNT AS VEGETABLE. CHILLI PEPPER AND HIGH-FAT, DEEP-FRY LEGUME ARE SECRET TO ANCESTOR LONG LIFE.

SAMBAL, KING OF SPICE (FUIYOH!)

Sambal is Southeast Asian people favorite condiment. Think of it like the OG sriracha. It disappear so quickly because it goes with EVERYTHING: any protein (including eggs), vegetable (sambal cover up flavor), noodles, and rice (fried, steamed, my coconut rice for Nasi Lemak on page 186), and so many other traditional dishes. Sometime Uncle Roger even put it on Western food like pizza, trust me. But the best thing about sambal is if you screw up a dish, use it to cover up your mistake. Everybody will say you are the best cook ever.

If any Western people are reading this, this paragraph is for you. (If you are Asian, skip this and go make one of my sambal recipes on the next pages.) Every sambal is NOT the same, haiyaa. The word is a generic term for Asian condiment made with fresh or dried chillies like my Sambal Belacan (page 66). That version is a simple chilli paste made from pounded fresh chillies, shrimp paste, and lime juice, so it more like a cross between what you Western people call salsa and hot sauce. Indonesian sambal oelek (the one every non-Asian think is the only sambal that exists because rooster brand with green lid in every grocery store condiment aisle) is also a "fresh" sambal with chillies but instead of lime juice, it have vinegar and sometime aromatics. The name *sambal tumis* (aka sambal nasi lemak, go to page 64 for Uncle Roger recipe) mean "slow cooked." That type of sambal is made with dried chillies and aromatics slowly fried in a LOT of oil to make it silky smooth and more like a rich, thick, oil-slicked condiment. (Mmmmm . . . so good.) Every region make each style differently.

SAMBAL TUMIS

(aka sambal nasi lemak. Asian people just say sambal, haiyaa . . .)

MAKES 1 GENEROUS CUP; SERVES 3 OR 4

You MUST serve this sambal with Nasi Lemak (page 184) or you are just eating Coconut Rice (page 186), not nasi lemak. (Sambal tumis last a whole month in refrigerator and it OK to make in blender, so Uncle Roger approve of doubling or tripling.)

Neutral oil, for frying

Fine table salt

MSG, King of Flavor

2 large mild dried chillies, guajillos or similar *(Length of your hand and two finger digits wide, this give sambal deep red color.)*

8 to 10 small dried RED chillies, like Thai jindas or chiles de árbol

1 small nub belacan (see page 27), about ¾ inch square and ¼ inch thick *(little bit more if you like sambal extra stinky)*

1 generous tablespoon seedless block tamarind (see page 28), softened in 3 tablespoons hot water *(This mean pull off nice chunk from block. Nobody measure.)*

5 to 6 long (pinky-length) FRESH red or green Thai chillies, sliced *(Red are best but green won't affect color because so many dried red chillies. Just don't be like Jamie Oliver. Leave ALL seeds in your fresh chilli.)*

7 to 8 garlic cloves

5 to 6 small Asian or 2 medium Western shallots, roughly chopped

1 stalk lemongrass, peeled, ends trimmed, and tender bottom half sliced

2-inch piece roughly chopped or shaved galangal (about 2 tablespoons)

About 2 tablespoons shaved gula melaka or jaggery (see page 25), or loosely packed dark brown sugar

---

Tear the large dried chillies into chunks and scrape out the seeds.

Soften both dried chillies in hot water for about 10 minutes. Leave the seeds in the small dried chillies or scrape out about half, if you want.

Heat a dry wok or small skillet until hot. Crumble the belacan over the wok. Toast the belacan, pressing down with the back of a spoon, until sand-like and lightened in color, about 3 minutes, then scrape into a dish.

Smash together the tamarind and soaking water with your fingers and push the paste firmly through a strainer. *(Use a cheap strainer like ancestor, too fine a sieve and you get no pulp. Or just pick out any seeds and bits of skin, easier.)*

(Uncle Roger is not up for more pounding today. So many dry chillies.) In a blender, combine the dried and fresh chillies, belacan, garlic, shallots, lemongrass, galangal, ½ teaspoon salt, 4 to 5 pinches of MSG, and 5 to 6 tablespoons water and blend until smooth. *(No big chunks of ingredient, haiyaa. Stop and stir, stop and stir.)*

In a wok, heat about 1 cup oil until hot. *(Don't skimp on oil. Need a LOT for pecah minyak, the "oil splitting" process.)* Reduce the heat to medium, add the chilli paste and gula melaka and fry the sambal until darkened in color and the oil separates from the aromatics, 20 to 25 minutes. After most of the water cooks off, stir regularly to keep the paste from burning. Turn off the heat and stir in 1 tablespoon of the tamarind pulp. Adjust the seasonings with tamarind, gula melaka, or salt.

Serve the sambal warm or at room temperature. *(Sambal should be covered in plenty of frying oil. Fat equals flavor. Save extra oil in wok!)*

Refrigerate the sambal in a jar or small container so the chilli paste is completely submerged in the frying oil for up to 1 month.

✓ FUIYOH!

After you eat all your sambal, keep leftover spicy oil make Uncle Roger's Special Fry Rice (page 46), nasi goreng (Indonesian and Malaysian-style fried rice, go search it up if you are Western), fried eggs, or to fry any other protein. Give everything BIG flavor.

UNCLE ROGER'S SAMBAL BELACAN

(Uncle Roger call this light sambal.)

MAKES 5 TO 6 TABLESPOONS, 3 TO 4 SERVINGS

(This sambal quick to make, pound in mortar only! No excuses. A little go a long way.)

This sambal is so light and fresh, all that Uncle Roger ever need. I cook some rice, make my Crispy Fried Egg (page 54), and make this sambal to give my rice bowl big flavor. Perfect quick meal. Always save any leftover for the next day, it a happy little surprise when you open up refrigerator.

Fine table salt

1 small nub belacan (see page 27), about ¾ inch square and ¼ inch thick *(Use feeling!)*

4 to 6 long (pinky-length) Thai red chillies *(red best, but green OK because not too many; don't be weak and scrape out seeds, haiyaa . . .)*

A big handful (about ½ cup) roughly chopped moderately spicy RED chillies, like cayennes, jalapeños, Fresnos, or serranos *(These are for red color only so, Uncle Roger usually remove the seeds but up to you.)*

¼ teaspoon granulated sugar

Juice of 1 to 2 key limes or ½ medium Western lime

Heat a dry wok or small skillet until hot. Crumble the belacan over the wok. Toast the belacan, pressing down with the back of a spoon, until sand-like and lightened in color, 2 to 3 minutes, then scrape into a dish. *(This step gonna be so pungent, will scare off neighbor.)*

In a large mortar, pound both chillies to a coarse paste. Add the belacan, sugar, and a pinch of salt and keep pounding until fairly smooth. *(Don't even think about using a blender, haiyaa. Too few ingredient and this such a small pounding job. If you broke your arm, that the only excuse for not pounding. Spice grinder that can handle wet ingredient work OK.)*

Just before serving, squeeze about 1 tablespoon of lime juice over the sambal. Adjust the seasonings with more lime juice or salt.

The sambal is best served the day it is made but can be refrigerated for a day or two and refreshed with another splash of lime juice.

✗ HAIYAA . . .

No green chillies! This is not salsa verde. Sambal is always RED. Asian market should have whatever medium-spicy chilli that is available locally. Where Uncle Roger live, usually red Fresno or jalapeño, and in UK, cayenne pepper.

✓ FUIYOH!

Uncle Roger like key limes but if don't have, Western lime also good. Calamansi (also called Filipino limes) are traditional in sambal but must be more green, less ripe. Once fruit turns orange it get too sweet.

THAI GREEN PAPAYA SALAD

(Som Tum)

SERVES 2 OR 3

Hot Thai auntie pounding papaya salad on street in giant mortar just for Uncle Roger make him feel so special. Next time niece and nephew in Northern Thailand, try local version with tiny raw salted field crabs. That Uncle Roger favorite. This is classic version, also delicious.

Dressing should be very thin! Uncle Roger still have nightmare about salad dressing after watching Gordon Ramsay f—k up som tum. Supposed to be liquid pooling at bottom of salad, not so thick and chunky. (British people turn everything into marmalade.) And never separate the dressing! Vegetable on plate, then dressing on top very Western thing to do. Asian people, we not into segregation like that. We mix everything up together, make everybody happy.

MSG, King of Flavor

VEGETABLES

Three large handfuls (about 3 cups packed) of shaved green papaya *(see technique, page 70)*

1 large thick carrot, peeled

2 or 3 long beans, trimmed

1 juicy medium tomato *(no heirloom tomato, hayiaa . . .)*

DRESSING

About 2 generous tablespoons seedless block tamarind (see page 28), softened in about 5 tablespoons hot water *(Just rip off nice big chunk of tamarind.)*

2 or 3 long (pinky-length) red or green Thai chillies

2 garlic cloves

A handful (about 6 tablespoons) of Fried Peanuts *(page 91; OK to toast peanut if short on time.)*

1 rounded tablespoon small dried salted shrimp

About 2 tablespoons shaved coconut or palm sugar, or loosely packed light brown sugar

About 2½ tablespoons fish sauce *(Use feeling!)*

4 or 5 key limes or 2 medium Western limes *(Need 2 to 3 tablespoons juice plus some of green peel, but only Western people measure.)*

TO SERVE

Steamed sticky rice *(Remember, sticky rice always served with som tum.)*

Recipe continues

DRESSING *(Niece and nephew, go read page 75 on kok and sak before start pounding . . .)*

Smash together the tamarind paste and soaking water with your fingers and push the paste firmly through a strainer, then add another 3 to 4 tablespoons water. *(Uncle Roger pull out my old strainer for this. Nothing with very tight mesh or get no pulp, but unstrained paste have too much fiber, haiyaa. Taste your tamarind water, must be very tangy. Add more paste if you want.)*

In a large mortar, pound the chillies and garlic into small pieces. *(No rimming with your pestle! In and out.)* Add about three-quarters of the peanuts, the dried shrimp, and sugar and pound until the peanuts are coarsely ground. Add the fish sauce, 6 spoonfuls (about 6 tablespoons) tamarind water, 2 tablespoon lime juice, and the leftover peel of 1 key lime or ½ Western lime. *(Throw whole lime into mortar after you squeeze out juice.)* Add 3 to 4 pinches of MSG and pound the lime several times to release the oils. *(A little more gentle pounding this time to keep juices in mortar.)* Adjust the seasonings with tamarind water, fish sauce, lime juice, sugar, or MSG; the dressing should be very intensely flavored. *(Thai auntie make papaya salad however niece and nephew like it. Sweeter or more sour, saltier, tangier. Now you get to do the same.)*

Add the long beans and carrots to the mortar and smash to open up the beans. Add the papaya and tomato wedges and smash again to bruise the papaya flesh and release the tomato juices. While pounding, scrape the bottom of the mortar with a large spoon to incorporate the dressing into the papaya flesh. *(This the same ancestor technique Niece Ae use when she make her Lao Papaya Salad on page 73. Watch her weejio.)* Remove the lime peel.

Scrape the salad into wide, shallow bowls and pour the dressing all over the salad. *(Vegetables should be sitting in POOL of dressing. No dry Western tom som!)* In the mortar, smash the remaining peanuts until coarsely ground and scatter them over the salad.

Serve the green papaya salad with the sticky rice.

VEGETABLES

Have all your vegetable ready before make dressing. Start by pounding your papaya, so satisfying.

Slice the carrot in half crosswise and then cut it into very thin slabs. Stack the slabs and cut them into matchsticks roughly the same size as the papaya. *(Asian people already know what matchstick cut is, haiyaa. Don't need instruction.)*

Cut the long beans into thumb-size pieces and the tomato into 6 to 8 wedges and set aside both in separate piles.

How to ~~Shave~~ Mutilate a Green Papaya

(LIKE A BADASS THAI OR LAO AUNTIE)

You can fuk (pound and chop) your papaya a day ahead and keep in refrigerator tightly covered. Now ready to make Uncle Roger favorite Thai papaya salad (page 67) or Niece Ae's Lao version. (Uncle Roger doesn't need to keep giving you the page number for everything, just turn the page for hers.)

Start with 1 large green papaya (2 to 2½ pounds) to make 3 to 4 cups packed shaved papaya.

First, peel the papaya. *(Why looking for fancy peeler in kitchen drawer? So Western. Just use knife, haiyaa.)*

(If you aren't good at air-chopping like Asian aunties, skip to Western version. Best not to go to hospital.) Hold the papaya in one hand while you quickly pound all over the top half with a sharp knife. Keep going back and forth over the surface of one side the papaya to make a lot of long, thin cuts very close to one another. *(Papaya can handle hard pounding. Need deep enough cuts so can shave off slices.)* Turn the knife on its side and run the blade from the top to the bottom of the fruit to shave off long, thin strips. Rotate the papaya and keep pounding and shaving all sides. When only thicker pieces can be shaved off, pound the papaya some more before slicing again; stop when you get to the pithy core.

(This version is for Western people . . .) Cut off one end of the papaya and lay the papaya on a work surface to pound it as instructed above. Stand the papaya upright to shave off long, thin strips. Thinly slice any larger shavings that didn't fully separate into shards. *(Or just throw bad strips on floor like Uncle Roger.)*

How to Slice and Juice a Lime

(Western way to slice lime is so wasteful, haiyaa. Thai people know how to get out ALL of juice.) Roll the lime around on the counter a few times with the palm of your hand. *(Give lime a little massage. Help soften it up so all juice squirt out.)* Slice off one end. Stand the lime upright and slice it into 3 or 4 pieces so the middle stays intact. *(This mean you are leaving the core.)* To juice the lime, push the edge of the spoon into the flesh of each wedge and press the lime around the spoon. *(See how much juice you get with proper slicing technique?)*

Weejios

Uncle Roger Review Gordon Ramsay Thai Papaya Salad

Uncle Roger Cancelled by Another Country (*Watch Auntie @AeBayBayy show off her papaya chop skills, FUIYOH!*)

NIECE AE'S LAO PAPAYA SALAD

(Thum Mak Hoong)

SERVES 2 OR 3 ASIAN PEOPLE *(Uncle Roger scared to serve this to Western people, they might die from all the extra spicy chilli pepper. Go make Thai papaya salad on page 67. It milder.)*

When Uncle Roger do weejio and say, "Lao food like shit version of Thai food," I get all kind of hate comment DM. Even death threat. Uncle Roger get one angry weejio from a Lao niece, Ae Southammavong. (Ae still working on her Auntie title. Make very good thum mak hoong but such a nasty mouth.) In her weejio, Niece Ae say she make Lao food that will be so spicy, afterward Uncle Roger "ass be so hot, your ladyboy can feel it too after she done with you." (Uncle Roger hope children don't know what that mean. If they do, that their parent fault.)

How could Uncle Roger turn down such nice offer? This the most interaction I ever had with any woman. I pack my stuff, fly all the way to the capital of Laos, Minneapolis, just to meet Niece Ae and make her Lao papaya salad.

MSG, King of Flavor

VEGETABLES

3 large handfuls (about 3 cups packed) of shaved green papaya (see technique, page 70)

1 juicy medium tomato, or a handful of cherry tomatoes

DRESSING

2 generous tablespoons seedless block tamarind (see page 28), softened in about 5 tablespoons hot water *(Nobody measure, even Niece Ae just rip off big piece of tamarind.)*

4 to 6 long (pinky-length) red or green Thai chillies *(Niece Ae try to kill Uncle Roger with big handful chillies. OK in some dish but in little salad, a lot.)*

1 garlic clove

About 1 tablespoon shaved coconut or palm sugar, or loosely packed light brown sugar

About 1 tablespoon fish sauce

1½ tablespoons fermented fish sauce *(Regular fish sauce not the same! This special Lao version called padaek or pla ra, read my note.)*

½ teaspoon fermented black crab paste *(nam pu; this give Lao version extra funky smell.)*

½ teaspoon shrimp paste

4 to 5 key limes or 2 medium Western limes *(Need 2 to 3 tablespoons juice plus some of green peel, but only Western people measure.)*

TO SERVE

Steamed sticky rice *(Must be sticky rice, use as utensil. Cook in steamer basket like Lao auntie or OK to use rice cooker.)*

Recipe continues

VEGETABLES

(Did you peel and air-chop your green papaya like Uncle Roger show you for Thai Green Papaya Salad recipe? Uncle Roger been practicing my fuk skills since weejio. Don't think dirty niece and nephew. Fuk is Lao word for chop.)

Cut the tomato into 6 to 8 wedges or the cherry tomatoes in half. *(Air-slice like Thai auntie, cutting board so wasteful.)*

DRESSING

(Read Uncle Roger note on mortar and pestle, kok and sak, before start.) Smash together the tamarind paste and soaking water with your fingers and push the paste firmly through a strainer, then add another 3 to 4 tablespoons water. *(Tamarind water must be very smooth for salad dressing so Uncle Roger always use my old strainer. Remember, don't use a fancy fine-mesh French sieve or you will be pounding tamarind through it for ten minutes.)*

In a large mortar, pound the chillies, garlic, and sugar until smashed into small pieces. Add both fish sauces, crab paste, shrimp paste, 6 spoonfuls (about 6 tablespoons) tamarind water, 2 tablespoons lime juice *(Use feeling!)*, and the leftover peel of 1 key lime or ½ Western lime. *(Throw whole lime into mortar after you squeeze out juice.)* Add 3 to 4 pinches of MSG and pound the lime several times to release the oils. *(A little more gentle pounding this time to keep juices in mortar.)* Adjust the seasonings with lime juice, fish sauce *(regular fish sauce this time)*, or MSG; the dressing should be intensely flavored. *(Smell of fish sauce, stinky crab paste, and spicy chillies will scare off all your white neighbor.)*

Add three large handfuls (about 3 cups packed) papaya and the tomatoes and smash to bruise the papaya flesh and release the tomato juices. While pounding, scrape the bottom of the mortar with a large spoon to incorporate the dressing into the papaya flesh as you pound it. *(Smash down with pestle, then scoop up, like Niece Ae do in weejio.)* Remove the lime peel.

TO SERVE

Scrape the salad into wide, shallow bowls and pour the dressing all over the salad. *(Vegetables should be sitting in POOL of dressing. This not Western salad, haiyaa.)* Serve the green papaya salad with the sticky rice. *(Lao people use sticky rice as utensil. Pick up rice, then pick up salad. Shove into mouth in one bite. No chopstick, or Uncle Roger get canceled. Again.)*

Weejios

Uncle Roger Cancelled by Another Country (*Niece @AeBayBayy show Uncle Roger papaya pound-and-slice technique.*)

Uncle Roger Almost Died: 24 Hours in Thailand (*Lao papaya salad frm hawker @MarkWiens take me to was SO spicy.*)

× HAIYAA . . .

No substitutions! Uncle Roger can't handle any more yelling from Niece Ae, she so loud.

✓ FUIYOH!

Lao ingredient hard to find except where Lao people live—Laos and Minneapolis. In US, niece and nephew can usually order fermented fish sauce and black crab paste (and a nice kok and sak) from shopsoutheats.com, online store run by nice Southeast Asian auntie. Niece Ae need to take customer service lesson from her, stop yelling at Uncle Roger, haiyaa.

KOK AND SAK

Lao and Thai clay mortar is called kok. (Don't think dirty!) Have smoother surface to break apart ingredients gently, instead of smashing them to a paste. Very important: Must use wood pestle, called sak, with clay mortar. Lao and Thai people do so much pounding, if pestle made of hard clay or granite, break mortar. If only have granite or other rough, hard mortar, use wooden spoon to more gently pound ingredients for both Lao and Thai papaya salad.

FERMENTED FISH SAUCE (PADAEK)

Label usually say "ground preserved fish" because this is unfiltered fish sauce. Made with freshwater fish, not anchovy like most fish sauce. Lao fish sauce is very thick, and more sour and smelly than Thai or Vietnamese fish sauce. Pantai brand most common in West.

FERMENTED BLACK CRAB PASTE (NAM PU)

Not the same as Thai red crab paste! Sometime label say crab extract but what you want is nam pu. Lao people make it from fermented guts of black rice paddy crab (mmm, delicious). Even more stinky than Lao fish sauce.

FUCHKA

(Bengali version of pani puri; no, it is not pronounced fucka . . .)

MAKES 50 TO 60 FUCHKA; SERVES 8 TO 12 AS AN APPETIZER

(Yes you want to make this many. Everybody think they will only eat a few fuchka. Uncle Roger could eat 10 as snack. Perfect for party.)

Pronounced fooj-kah. Uncle Roger so excited when Nephew Nigel invite me to his wedding. I get to eat so much good food, like Auntie Shakila's fuchka, the Bengali version of Indian pani puri. (Auntie Shakila is Nephew Nigel's mother-in-law.) Uncle Roger stand by food table all night, stuffing each little semolina puff with potato and chana dal (split yellow chickpea) filling and all the topping. Pour sweet and sour tamarind water and some of Auntie Shakila's cilantro water into puff, shove the whole thing in my mouth for BIG explosion of flavor. Very good cover tactic while I check out eligible aunties.

The cilantro pani is optional, but I like a little with the tamarind for a nice flavor. With store-bought pani puri, you need to fry or toast them so they taste fresh. —Auntie Shakila

50 to 60 (6 to 7 ounces) packaged pani puri *(Get extra package, shells easy to break when you toast or fry them.)*

Chana Dal and Potato Filling (recipe follows)

Tamarind Pani (recipe follows)

Auntie Shakila's Cilantro Pani (recipe follows)

Make the filling and tamarind and cilantro pani a day or two ahead, you ready to party with Uncle Roger.

TOPPINGS

(Just chop up plenty of each topping. Nobody measure, haiyaa.)

4 Boiled Eggs (page 151; *firm yolk, 11 minute)*

4 small cucumbers *(If use big cucumber, peel first and scrape out seeds.)*

2 to 3 juicy medium tomatoes, seeds removed

1 medium red onion

Two handfuls (about 1 cup) of cilantro leaves

A handful (about ½ cup) of moderately spicy green chillies, seeded *(Jwala, serrano, or green cayenne; jalapeño only if you weak. Thai chilli also good, little spicier.)*

Recipe continues

Preheat the oven to 350°F (180°C). *(Auntie Shakila fry her pani puri shell for a few seconds on each side in hot oil. Uncle Roger like to toast my shells, pani puri already fried so less greasy, and easy.)*

Arrange the pani puri shells on a baking sheet and bake for about 5 minutes. *(Don't overbake, this just to refresh shells.)* If not using within an hour, cover the cooled shells to keep out moisture. *(Just put back in box, haiyaa. Don't waste plastic wrap or bag.)*

TOPPINGS

(Leave your pea and potato filling and tamarind and cilantro water in refrigerator until ready to serve. Must be cold!)

Grate the eggs on the largest holes of a box grater. *(Best method, nice texture, but you can finely chop.)* Chop the cucumbers, tomatoes, onion, cilantro, and green chillies and keep each in separate piles. *(Not too big, haiyaa. Pieces must fit in little pani puri shell.)*

TO SERVE

Set out each of the fuchka components so everyone can assemble their own: the pani puri shells, pea-potato filling, eggs, cucumbers, tomatoes, onions, cilantro, and green chillies. Pour the tamarind pani and cilantro pani into glasses or small pitchers. *(Put little spoon in both pani so people can stir to reincorporate ingredients.)*

(If you don't know how to eat fuchka, flick top of pani puri shell with finger to poke hole in top. Put a SMALL spoonful or two of pea and potato filling in shell, 2 teaspoon max. Need to leave room for topping and tamarind water. Now get a tiny bit of whatever topping you like. Pour in enough tamarind water to almost fill shell and add a little cilantro water if you want. Out at restaurant, everybody just dunk filled pani puri in the herb pani and shove shell into mouth, but Uncle Roger trying to use proper wedding etiquette. Drizzle a little on top with pretty spoon. Pop fuchka in mouth before shell gets soggy!)

AUNTIE SHAKILA'S CILANTRO PANI

This count as all your vegetable for the week. Green smoothie, very healthy.

Makes about 2 cups, enough for the Fuchka (page 77)

Fine table salt

Two big handfuls (about 1 cup fairly packed) of roughly chopped cilantro leaves and tender top stems

1½ tablespoons granulated sugar

1 to 2 large lemons

In a blender, combine the cilantro, sugar, and 2 pinches of salt. *(This time no black salt, regular.)* With the blender running, slowly add ½ cup water and blend until smooth. Add the juice of 1 lemon (about 2 tablespoons) and another 1½ cups water. *(Use feeling, taste cilantro pani as you add water.)*

Refrigerate the cilantro pani overnight or up to 3 days. Before serving, adjust the seasonings with sugar or lemon juice. *(Not too much lemon, remember will have the tamarind pani. Cilantro pani soften flavor.)*

Recipe continues

CHANA DAL AND POTATO FILLING

Remember, need to make the filling, and both the cilantro and tamarind pani, a day or two before you want to serve Fuchka (page 77).

Makes about 2½ cups, enough for the Fuchka

Finely ground black salt (kala namak; see page 87) and fine table salt

SPICE MIX

1 tablespoon cumin seeds

2 small dried red chillies, like Thai jindas or chiles de árbol

FILLING

½ cup chana dal, soaked overnight and drained *(Indian split yellow chickpea not the same size or variety as big chickpea or Western split pea, haiyaa.)*

½ teaspoon ground turmeric

⅛ teaspoon baking soda

2 to 3 medium red or yellow potatoes (about ½ pound), peeled and cut into large bite-size chunks

SPICE MIX

In a dry skillet, toast the cumin seeds until fragrant and scrape into a dish. *(Niece and nephew know how to do this by now. Toast in dry skillet until fragrant, a minute or two.)* Toast the chillies. *(Same process as cumin seed, throw in skillet, toast chilli on both side until smell good but not burnt.)*

In a mortar, pound the cumin seeds to a powder or grind in a spice grinder. *(Scrape into separate dish.)*

Grind the toasted chillies in the mortar or spice grinder, add ¾ teaspoon of the ground toasted cumin, ¼ teaspoon black salt, and 2 pinches of table salt. *(Save this spice mix for your pea and potato filling and the rest of the ground cumin for the Tamarind Pani, page 81. Uncle Roger trying to save time, toast enough for both now.)*

FILLING

In a medium pot, combine the chana dal, turmeric, baking soda, ¼ teaspoon table salt, and enough water to cover the peas by 1 finger joint (about 1 inch). Bring to a low boil, partly cover the pot, and cook until the peas are tender, about 20 minutes; if the water ever reaches below the level of the chana dal, add enough to cover them. Drain the peas and set aside.

In the pot, combine the potatoes, ½ teaspoon salt, and enough water just to cover the potatoes. *(Or just use another pot, cook while pea also cooking on stove.)* Bring to a low boil and cook the potatoes until very tender, about 10 minutes. *(Use feeling, not the kitchen timer. Poke potato with chopstick.)* Drain and transfer the potatoes to a large bowl. When cool enough to handle, smash the potatoes with your hands. *(Should be nicely smashed with little pieces of potato only! Remember, must fit in pani puri shell with other topping.)*

Add the chana dal to the potatoes, gently mix with your hands to combine. Sprinkle the chilli-cumin spice mixture over the filling and mix again. Refrigerate the filling overnight or up to 3 days. Before serving, adjust the seasonings with cumin or black salt or table salt.

× HAIYAA . . .

No substitute for black salt (page 87)!

CHANA DAL

This is cute tiny baby chickpea, split in half, why called "split chickpea" on package. Made from small dark chickpea variety called kala chana. (Don't want whole kala chana for this recipe, only split. Get at Indian market.) Brown skin removed before chickpea split in half so have nice yellow color. Don't substitute Western yellow split pea or lentil (will turn into mushy baby food) or kabuli chana, the bigger chickpea variety used in Middle Eastern food. Not same variety of chickpea and too big!

TAMARIND PANI

Tamarind pani should be very thin (why it is called tamarind water) but have a strong, tangy flavor. Need enough tamarind to make you pucker and balance the potato and pea filling. Best to make tamarind water a day or two ahead so flavors develop. Black salt is how you know it authentic, can smell the sulfur when you take it out of refrigerator and open the lid.

Makes about 4 cups, plenty for the Fuchka *(page 77)*

Finely ground black salt (kala namak, see page 87) and fine table salt

5 to 6 ounces seedless block tamarind (see page 28; *need big piece, little bigger than deck of cards. Don't waste time, get seedless block!)*

About 2 teaspoons granulated sugar *(Jaggery is traditional, also good, but must melt in water first.)*

Toasted ground cumin, reserved from making the spice mix for Chana Dal and Potato Filling *(about 1¼ teaspoons but nobody measure; if you forgot to save some, make more)*

½ to 1 teaspoon chaat masala *(as much as you want, but chaat masala mix usually have a little black salt, so start with less)*

In a bowl, break up the tamarind into chunks and completely cover the pieces with 1¼ cups hot water. When cool enough to handle, smash up the tamarind with your hands. *(This is not the time to be gentle. Really go at it.)* Strain the tamarind through a fine-mesh sieve, pushing down on the pulp; you should have about ¾ cup of tamarind paste. *(Even with "seedless" pulp, worth it to take the time to strain tamarind this time in a fine-mesh sieve because seedless pulp still have coarse bits of skin. Nobody want to drink gritty tamarind water.)*

In a large jar or bowl, combine ½ cup plus 2 to 3 tablespoons tamarind paste *(so specific this cookbook, haiyaa, use feeling . . .)*, the sugar, reserved toasted ground cumin, chaat masala, 3 to 4 pinches of black salt, ½ teaspoon table salt, and 3 cups water and mix well. Adjust the seasonings with the tamarind paste, sugar, chaat masala, black salt, or table salt. *(Tamarind pani should have BIG flavor, add as much tangy paste and spices as you like.)* Refrigerate the tamarind water overnight or up to 1 week; refrigerate the extra softened tamarind paste to readjust the tanginess again before serving. *(Rest time for tamarind water let black salt flavors develop.)*

GADO GADO

SERVES 2 *(Three or four people if you are like Uncle Roger and only eat little bit of vegetable. Have enough peanut sauce to double recipe, serve whole big family if you want.)*

Gado gado is daily Indonesian food, nobody need to oversell this like Jamie Oliver. He call this a "supercharged salad," haiyaa. Reminds me of every real estate agent—always exaggerating. Every auntie make gado gado her own way, this is just one variation that Uncle Roger like. And it brings sad vegetable in refrigerator back to life. Blanch limp vegetable in hot water, it spring right back. (Sorry, children.)

Neutral oil, for frying

MSG, King of Flavor

A MIX OF BLANCHED VEGETABLES, LIKE:

4 or 5 long beans, trimmed and cut into thumb-size pieces

½ medium chayote squash, cored and cut into wedges

Two handfuls of mung bean sprouts

Three handfuls of water spinach or similar variety *(read Uncle Roger note)*, tough ends trimmed and rinsed well to remove any grit

Two handfuls of Chinese (napa) cabbage, cut into long strips

2 medium red or yellow potatoes, peeled and cut into bite-size pieces

FRIED TOFU AND TEMPEH

4 slices pressed tofu, drained *(Firm tofu only as last resort, read at end of recipe.)*

3 to 4 slices tempeh

TO SERVE

1 to 2 small or ½ large cucumber, peeled and sliced *(For big cucumber, scrape out seed with spoon.)*

1 juicy medium tomato, cut into wedges

1 to 2 Boiled Eggs *(page 151; soft boiled with jammy-firm yolk, 7 to 8 minute! Don't overcook or yolk dry out, haiyaa.)*

About ¾ cup Kuah Kacang *(page 85; this about half the sauce, save the rest for later in week.)*

Keropok *(fish or shrimp crackers; see page 128)*

BLANCHED VEGETABLES *(Order you boil not so important but always boil potatoes last. They make the water starchy.)*

Fill a pot or wok halfway with water and bring to a low boil. Blanch the vegetables and transfer to a platter with chopsticks, a spider, or tongs. *(Read times below if need help. And remember! Only Western people use strainer or colander and ice bath, haiyaa. Waste of time and water.)* Keep the vegetables in separate piles and bring the water back to a boil before blanching the next vegetable. *(Proper cookbook have so much instruction. Just boil vegetable, haiyaa.)*

- **LONG BEANS:** 1½ to 2 minutes, until crisp-tender
- **CHAYOTE:** 4 to 5 minutes, until tender but not falling apart
- **BEAN SPROUTS:** About 30 seconds, until crisp-tender
- **SPINACH:** 10 to 15 seconds for water spinach, around 30 seconds for most other spinach, just until wilted *(Squeeze out extra water after cook. Don't kill spinach like French. Cook so long, lose freshness, they have to cover up mistake with cream and butter.)*
- **CABBAGE:** 1 to 1½ minutes, until the leaves are wilted and the stalks are crisp-tender
- **POTATOES:** 5 to 8 minutes, depending on the size, until tender but not falling apart

Recipe continues

FRIED TOFU AND TEMPEH

Wrap the tofu in a kitchen towel and lay a can of food on top for about 15 minutes to remove more moisture, then pat dry. *(If you bought correct Indonesian pressed tofu, don't need to dry in towel or press. Food company already did better job than you ever could.)*

Cut the tofu and tempeh into bite-size pieces and season with 3 to 4 pinches of MSG.

Heat a wok until hot. Add about 2 tablespoons neutral oil and swirl to evenly coat the surface. Fry the tofu until golden brown on all sides and transfer to a plate.

Add another splash of oil to the wok and fry the tempeh until golden brown. *(OK, ready to eat!)*

TO SERVE

Arrange the blanched vegetables in piles on a large serving platter. Tuck the cucumber, tomatoes, tofu, tempeh, and eggs, around the vegetables. *(Take time to make it pretty!)* Spoon the kuah kacang generously over the salad. *(This not Western salad. Need a LOT of peanut sauce and pour it ALL over salad. Do not mix! Make vegetables soggy.)*

Serve the gado gado with the keropok.

✔ FUIYOH!

Uncle Roger love when Asian ingredient confuse Western people. Water spinach actually not spinach but different plant that grow in water with long hollow stalk and thin leaves. So delicious. Called kangkong (Indonesian/Malaysian), ong choy (Chinese), phak bung (Thai), rau muong (Vietnamese), and kuushinsa (Japanese). One called Taiwan spinach that have bigger leaf (look more like Western spinach but with sweeter flavor) is also Uncle Roger–approved. If only have Western spinach, get big leaf variety, not tiny spinach in bag with no flavor.

Deep-fried keropok get umami flavor from fish or shrimp. Keep in pantry for gado gado or for Uncle Roger mum famous Sarawak Acar (page 126).

PRESSED TOFU

Can't just press out water from Japanese firm silken tofu and call it pressed tofu like Western recipe say to do, haiyaa. Real pressed tofu have chewy, dense texture. Go to Thai or Indonesian market, they will have right tofu. Even some fancy expensive Western market sell pressed tofu from American company like Melissa's. ONLY if extra-firm silken tofu all you can find, OK to press out water yourself. But it is NOT Uncle Roger–approved, texture all wrong.

KUAH KACANG

(This is NOT peanut butter sauce, haiyaa.)

MAKES ABOUT 1¾ CUPS

Kuah kacang for gado gado different depending on region where it is made. (And not the same as kuah kacang for satay, haiyaa. Have to make different kind of peanut sauce, get my recipe on page 201.) This version is Uncle Roger favorite. Based on traditional style from Java, where the salad was invented. It doesn't have coconut milk like some recipe from other parts of Indonesia but still a little bit of nice sweetness. Niece and nephew, remember this called peanut SAUCE. No peanut butter! This not PB&J!

Neutral oil, for frying *(use the leftover oil from frying the peanut, have best flavor)*

Fine table salt

MSG, King of Flavor

About 2 teaspoons seedless block tamarind (see page 28), softened in 1 tablespoon hot water *(How anybody supposed to measure 2 teaspoon from hard block tamarind, haiyaa. Just guess.)*

1 to 2 long (pinky-length) red or green Thai chilli, sliced *(Don't scrape out seeds!)*

1 Thai bird's eye chilli or another long Thai chilli, sliced

2 to 3 small Asian or 1 medium Western shallot, roughly chopped

1 to 2 garlic cloves, roughly chopped

1-inch piece roughly chopped or shaved galangal (about 1 tablespoon)

1-inch piece roughly chopped ginger (about 1 tablespoon)

1 cup Fried Peanuts (page 91; *OK to toast in oven but raw peanut must have skin for color!)*

About 1 tablespoon coconut or palm sugar, or loosely packed light brown sugar

2 to 3 makrut (kaffir) lime leaves, rolled and finely chopped, or 1 strip finely chopped lime peel *(Dried lime leaf too crumbly. Use lime peel, no bitter white pith.)*

About 3 tablespoons kecap manis

Smash together the tamarind and soaking water with your fingers and push the paste firmly through a strainer. *(No fine-mesh sieve! Holes too tiny, get no pulp. Want cheap strainer from Asian store, medium mesh.)*

Heat a wok until hot. Add about 2 tablespoons oil and swirl to evenly coat the surface. Reduce the heat to medium and stir-fry both chillies, shallots, garlic galangal, and ginger until softened, about 2 minutes. Scrape into a large mortar.

Recipe continues

Pound the chillies and aromatics to a coarse paste. *(OK, OK. If you don't have big mortar, throw ingredient into blender or food processor AFTER you pound chillies to get them nice and ground up first.)* Add the peanuts and tamarind pulp and pound to break up the peanuts. Add ½ cup water, keep pounding and scraping the bottom of the mortar until coarsely ground, then add another ½ cup water and pound until paste-like with some chunkier pieces. Add the sugar and lime leaves or peel and smash several times to release the oils from the lime leaves.

To the wok, add another spoonful (about 1 tablespoon) oil and reheat over medium heat. *(Not too hot, making sauce now.)* Scrape the ground peanut mixture into the wok, add the kecap manis, ½ teaspoon salt, 2 to 3 pinches of MSG, and ½ cup water and bring to a low boil. Cook the sauce, stirring regularly, until slightly darkened in color and somewhat thickened, about 15 minutes; if the sauce reduces too much as it cooks, add a little more water. *(Sauce should not be too thick, haiyaa. Remember peanut sauce for gado gado is like a very chunky salad dressing.)* Adjust the seasoning with kecap manis or salt.

Serve the kuah kacang warm.

Refrigerate any leftover sauce for up to 5 days. Rewarm over low heat.

KECAP MANIS

This Indonesian version of sweetened soy sauce is called sweet soy (soya) sauce on most bottles. Name come from *koechiap* ("sauce"), Cantonese word that later became ketchup in the West. (Western people steal *everything* from Asian people, then screw it up. Flavor nothing like ketchup.) Soy sauce is reduced down with palm sugar and sometimes other ingredient, then fermented until very thick, like molasses. Kecap manis balance the flavor of Kuah Kacang (Uncle Roger have a different version on page 201) and other Southeast Asian dishes.

Weejio

Uncle Roger FORCED to Review Jamie Oliver Indonesian Salad

CUCUMBER RAITA

MAKES ABOUT 2½ CUPS; SERVES A FAMILY

(That mean eight people, perfect amount for Auntie Shakila's Kacchi Biryani on page 208.)

Auntie Shakila (Nephew Nigel mother-in-law) make a classic cucumber raita that whole family love. Hers have a few pinches of mint, cilantro, ground coriander, and green chillies. (Not too much!) So cool and refreshing. Perfect side for biryani or anything that is little bit spicy. This can cool you down. It like yogurt on crack.

Finely ground black salt *(kala namak very important, special flavor)*

Finely ground white pepper

2 cups Indian dahi or other thick whole-milk yogurt like Greek

⅓ to ½ cup finely chopped peeled cucumber *(Very finely chop! Persian cucumber easy, don't need to remove seeds. If use big cucumber, scrape out seeds first.)*

1 to 2 long (pinky-length) green Thai chillies, seeds removed and chopped *(Or whatever green chilli you like, but remember, raita not meant to be spicy.)*

1 small spoonful (1 to 1½ teaspoons) finely chopped cilantro leaves *(Herb count as vegetable, not too many. Use feeling.)*

1 small spoonful (1 to 1½ teaspoons) finely chopped mint leaves

About 4 BIG pinches toasted ground coriander seeds *(Auntie Shakila always toast whole seed in dry skillet until it smell good, a minute or two, and grind fresh. Best flavor.)*

Put the dahi in a bowl. If using a thicker style of yogurt, thin it with just enough water to make it slightly thinner; it should be almost pourable. *(Greek yogurt usually so thick, must eat with a spoon. Raita should be like extra-thick milkshake. Best with spoon but can almost slurp.)* Fold in the cucumber, chillies, cilantro, mint, ground coriander, 2 to 3 pinches of black salt, and 4 to 5 pinches of white pepper. *(Not too much black salt. Smoky sulfur from volcanic ash very strong.)* Adjust the seasonings with ground coriander, black salt, or white pepper.

Refrigerate the raita for at least 30 minutes before serving. *(Raita is best eaten the same day. Cucumber get soggy, release too much water if make ahead.)*

BLACK SALT (KALA NAMAK)

This is secret ingredient in authentic raita, Fuchka (page 77), and other Indian food. Volcanic rock salt smoked in big oven with charcoal, herbs, and spices until salt melt. When cool, it have a smoky flavor and little bit of rotten egg smell from the sulfur. (Black salt smell bad, but it taste good. It the opposite of body wash.) No substitute!

UNCLE ROGER'S SPICY KIMCHI

MAKES ABOUT 5 CUPS

Uncle Roger like my kimchi hot and spicy but not too fermented. Sometimes kimchi get too sour, nobody want that. How sour depend on how long you leave kimchi to ferment, but also the ingredients you use. Start at room temperature, then move it to refrigerator where it will ferment more slowly. Never use gochujang paste like Western and fancy modern Asian recipe say! Real kimchi like ancestor make get spiciness from gochugaru, the Korean chilli flakes used to make gochujang. (Uncle Roger agree with ancestor, gochujang paste have too many other seasoning for good kimchi.) Uncle Roger learn a few tips from Auntie Maangchi; she very good kimchi maker. (She also make Kimchi Fry Rice that I review on page 50.)

Most Western people think there is just one style of kimchi, but so many different kinds and ways to make it. Some auntie like to add fermented shrimp with their fish sauce for bigger umami flavor. I like just fish sauce, a little milder. Maangchi make hers the traditional ancestor way, with a rice porridge. Uncle Roger too lazy to cook down rice porridge, and vegetable don't need it to ferment. Rice porridge jump-start the fermentation process so vegetable get a stronger taste faster. If you leave it out, kimchi will still ferment, just more slowly so a little less sour at first. I add a little sugar instead, it does the same thing and make my kimchi a little less tangy, more balanced—how I like it. And mine very quick to make, most of process happen in jar after you walk away. You can see that happening in the pretty photo. It was taken when my kimchi just start releasing bubbles and ferment after twenty-four hours, so still very fresh. In three to four more days, it will be ready (still mild), or let it ferment longer in the refrigerator for a more intense flavor.

SALTED CABBAGE AND VEGETABLES

Fine table salt

About ½ medium head Chinese (napa) cabbage, cored and sliced in half lengthwise

2 to 3 small Korean or 1 small daikon radish, peeled and cut into matchsticks *(Asian radish so many different sizes, tiny to huge. Need enough to make 1 cup matchsticks.)*

1 large thick carrot, peeled and cut into matchsticks

3 scallions, chopped *(Chop whole scallion for kimchi.)*

CHILLI PASTE

8 to 10 garlic cloves, finely chopped

2 to 3 small Asian or 1 medium Western shallot, diced

1-inch piece finely chopped ginger (about 1 tablespoon)

½ cup coarse or ⅓ cup finely ground gochugaru *(Check label, some fine ground, some little coarser flake, that what you want.)*

About 6 tablespoons fish sauce

1 tablespoon shaved coconut or palm sugar, or loosely packed light brown sugar, melted in 2 tablespoons hot water

Recipe continues

SALTED CABBAGE AND VEGETABLES

Chop the cabbage into large bite-size pieces or strips. *(However you like it, Uncle Roger like mine in nice-size chunks.)*

Transfer six large handfuls (about 6 cups packed) of cabbage to a colander; rinse and drain the cabbage but don't dry off the leaves. *(Colander so fancy, haiyaa. Put cabbage in bowl, cover with cold water, put palm of hand over cabbage leaves, hold on to them and dump out water.)* Sprinkle 1½ tablespoons salt over the cabbage and rub the leaves lightly with your hands to evenly distribute the salt. Set the cabbage aside for about 2 hours to allow the leaves to wilt. *(If use colander, leave colander in sink, liquid will drain off as it releases water. Go watch Uncle Roger weejio.)*

When the leaves have wilted, rinse the cabbage with cold water again and drain. Return the cabbage to the bowl and add the radishes, carrot, and scallions.

CHILLI PASTE

In a small dish, mix together the garlic, shallots, ginger, gochugaru, fish sauce, and sugar water. *(This mean your palm or other sugar and hot water.)* Massage the chilli paste all over the vegetables. *(Nobody need rubber gloves, haiyaa. We making kimchi, not having prostate exam.)* Adjust the seasonings with fish sauce.

Pack the kimchi into a large ceramic crock, an extra-large sterilized glass jar, or 2 smaller 1-quart (32-ounce) jars; leave a little room at the top. *(Use ancestor crock or very clean glass jar. Plastic container stain, haiyaa.)* Firmly press down to release any air pockets; the vegetables won't be fully submerged at this point. Loosely cover the jar with plastic wrap or a lid. *(Not too tight! Kimchi need to burp, get rid of excess CO_2.)*

Let the vegetables ferment at room temperature, out of direct sunlight, for about 3 days. *(Time depend on how warm or cool your kitchen.)* Open the lid once a day to burp the kimchi and push the vegetables further down into the liquid. When you press down, the liquid should release tiny air bubbles, which is a sign the fermentation process has started. The kimchi can be eaten now though it will still be very fresh tasting. *(Uncle Roger like to let my kimchi age a little longer in the fridge, at least a week. This give it a nice flavor and texture.)*

Refrigerate the kimchi, still loosely covered, for 2 to 3 months. It will continue to slowly ferment and gradually take on an increasingly sour flavor.

× HAIYAA . . .

No bitter Western cabbage or small, sad, tiny red radish. Must use Chinese cabbage and Korean or daikon radish!

Always cut vegetable for kimchi with knife, not cheese grater. Nobody want limp, flaccid vegetable.

Weejio

Uncle Roger Review Maangchi Kimchi Fried Rice (@Maangchi)

FRIED PEANUTS

(Kacang Goreng)

MAKES 1 TO 2 CUPS, OR HOWEVER MUCH YOU NEED

Fried peanut is KING. Southeast Asian version of health food, and Uncle Roger favorite snack. Peanut already packed with fat. Deep-fry in fat, make it even more delicious. FUIYOH!

Neutral oil, for deep-frying

1 to 2 cups (5 to 10 ounces) raw peanuts with skins *(Skin not optional! However much peanut you need, Uncle Roger always make more than I want to eat.)*

Line a plate, bowl, or tray with paper towels. Fill a wok with enough oil to cover the peanuts *(don't add peanut yet!)* and heat until very hot. *(Add 1 peanut or do chopstick test. Want fast, tiny bubbles.)* Deep-fry the peanuts until the skins darken slightly and the peanuts just begin to color, 1½ to 2 minutes; they should only be lightly colored and will continue to toast as they cool. *(Watch peanut closely! Taste peanut when cool. If burnt and bitter, throw out and start over, or give to American to turn into peanut butter.)* Scoop out the peanuts onto the paper towels.

Store the peanuts at room temperature in a tightly sealed bag or container for up to 1 week. *(Put little piece of paper towel in bag to soak up extra oil.)*

To toast the peanuts: *(ONLY when Uncle Roger short on time, I toast raw peanut. Flavor not as good and so healthy, haiyaa. But not bad.)* Toast the peanuts in a preheated 350°F (180°C) oven until the skins darken slightly and the peanuts just begin to color, 12 to 15 minutes; stir the peanuts occasionally as they toast. *(Watch closely after ten minutes, once peanut start to toast, burn quickly and taste bitter.)* Transfer the peanuts to a plate to cool.

✕ HAIYAA . . .

Why every Western store sell skinless, naked peanuts? Don't circumcise your peanut. Must use raw peanut with skin and fry at home for best flavor. Any good Southeast Asian market will have.

✓ FUIYOH!

Fry big batch of peanut, ready to make Thai Green Papaya Salad (page 67), Kuah Kacang (page 85) for Gado Gado (page 82), Nasi Lemak (page 184), Satay Sauce (page 201), and so many other Asian dishes.

Strain peanut fry oil, never throw away! So good in stir-fry or for whatever need extra flavor. Store in fridge for up to a few days.

Morning

ASIAN AMERICAN

ASIAN AMERICAN FOOD COMPLETELY DIFFERENT FROM ASIAN FOOD. THERE TOO MANY ASIAN AMERICAN DISHES THAT ARE WATERED DOWN, TOO SWEET, NO SPICE, NO MSG. (HAIYAA . . .) HERE HOW TO MAKE THEM THE RIGHT WAY. DON'T LET PANDA EXPRESS GET THEIR HANDS ON THIS.

OG UNCLE MARTIN YAN'S SHANGRI-LA BEEF

SERVES 4 OR 5 *(Don't just make one dish just for yourself, haiyaa. Chinese food meant to be shared family-style. That how you serve more people.)*

Martin Yan is Uncle Roger hero since I was young boy. Uncle Martin even sound like Uncle Roger, that why he the OG Uncle. He have cooking show that start all the way back in 1978, when only white people allowed on TV. Huge accomplishment. Remember, this back when everybody in the US afraid of two things: MSG and Asian people. Uncle Martin the first person to bring flavor to American television audience.

This recipe is based on recipe in *Best of Yan Can Cook*, Uncle Martin's thirty-sixth cookbook, only here you get special bonus tips just for niece and nephew. And Uncle Roger like a little more sauce on my Shangri-la beef, sauce pooling at the bottom, more for the rice. He really is the legend . . . next time Uncle Roger should call him Sifu Yan.

Neutral oil, for stir-frying

Finely ground white pepper and fine table salt

MSG, King of Flavor *(not Uncle Martin approved . . .)*

MARINATED BEEF

About 1¼ pounds flank steak

2 tablespoons soy sauce

2 tablespoons Chinese dark soy sauce

2 tablespoons Shaoxing rice wine

2 tablespoons cornstarch

STIR-FRY

5 to 6 garlic cloves

1 medium yellow or white onion

1 medium sweet red bell pepper

1 medium jicama *(Jicama come in very small to giant size, need 1 cup cut into matchstick.)*

3 scallions

A handful (about 15) of small dried red chillies, like Thai jindas or chiles de árbol

2 tablespoons Chinese chilli bean paste (doubanjiang)

2 tablespoons hoisin sauce

TO SERVE

Steamed rice

Recipe continues

MARINATED BEEF

Slice the beef against the grain into fairly thin but meaty strips; the slices should be thick enough to pick up with chopsticks. *(No slivers! All pieces should be about length of your index finger.)*

In a bowl, mix together the soy sauce, dark soy sauce, rice wine, cornstarch, 3 to 4 pinches of white pepper, and 2 to 3 pinches of salt. *(Now is the time Uncle Roger add 3 to 4 BIG pinch of MSG.)* Coat the meat evenly in the marinade.

STIR-FRY

(Proper vegetable prep very important for Chinese stir-fry! Slice your vegetable fast, like you running late for airport. "Tak-tak-tak-tak-tak." Uncle Roger love sound of cleaver chopping. So relaxing . . .)

Mince the garlic. *(With cleaver! Go watch Uncle Martin's weejio and see his amazing technique. You probably can't replicate it but fun to try.)* Scrape the garlic off to one side of the cutting board.

Slice off both ends of the onion. *(Hack, hack with your cleaver.)* Slice the onion in half lengthwise, then slice each half at an angle to make wedged-shaped pieces roughly ½ inch thick. *(No onion rings! Onion sliced into wedges for stir-fry impress all the aunties. You real chef now.)*

Slice off both ends of the bell pepper and scrape out the seeds and membranes. *(Watch weejio, see how to seesaw cleaver to clean inside of whole pepper at same time. So easy, even Uncle Roger can do it.)* Slice the pepper into strips roughly ½ inch wide and 2 finger joints (2 inches) long.

Cut the jicama into a rectangle, then slice into matchsticks roughly the same size as the bell peppers. *(You know how to do this, want about 1 cup jicama.)* Set the jicama aside with the garlic, onions, and bell pepper. *(Uncle Martin like to make so much noise in kitchen, tap his cleaver on counter every time he transfer vegetable to plate. So dramatic. Just put pepper in pile with onion and garlic.)*

Slice the scallions at a diagonal into 4 or 5 pieces and reserve in a separate pile.

Just before stir-frying, drizzle a little oil (about 2 teaspoons) over the meat and toss to combine. Do the same with the vegetables. *(This Uncle Martin trick to "lubricate" ingredients so don't stick inside too dry a wok. Sorry, children.)*

Heat a wok until hot. Add about 2 tablespoons oil and swirl to evenly coat the surface. *(Hot wok + cold oil = WOK HEI!)* Spread out the beef and chillies in a single layer and sear for about 10 seconds. *(Don't stir yet, haiyaa. Want to sear a few seconds to seal in juices.)* Toss and stir-fry the beef until barely pink in the center, about 1 minute. *(Use feeling, time depend on how thick meat.)* Scrape the beef onto a plate.

If the wok is dry, add another splash of oil. When hot, add the garlic, onions, bell pepper, and jicama and toss and stir for about 1 minute. Add the scallions and keep stirring and tossing until the yellow onions just begin to brown on the edges, about 30 seconds. *(No color yet? Wok not hot enough, haiyaa. That OK, keep cooking longer. Might take a few minutes.)* Add the chilli bean paste, hoisin sauce, beef and any meat-pan juices, and ½ cup water. *(Uncle Martin add a splash of water at end to add moisture, watch weejio. Uncle Roger like a little more water for all the extra sauce I make.)* Stir and toss the wok a few more times to coat the meat and vegetables evenly in the sauce.

Scrape the stir-fry onto plates and serve with the steamed rice.

CHINESE DOUBANJIANG (ALSO CALLED TOBAN-DJAN OR DOUBAN)

Fermented broad bean with chilli pepper even available in 1980s when OG Uncle Martin publish his first cookbooks. That mean it easy to find today, so don't pretend you don't have a jar for this recipe. Lee Kum Kee brand that can get most places is Uncle Roger–approved. (They call their version "chilli bean sauce" in English.)

Weejios

Uncle Roger Roasted by LEGEND Martin Yan

Uncle Roger Review OG Uncle Mongolian Beef (@ChefMartinYan)

UNCLE DIMSIMLIM'S CRISPY ORANGE CHICKEN

SERVES 4 OR 5 *(Only make as much as want to eat. Leftover get soggy, haiyaa.)*

When Chinese people come to America, they tell Western people what they are buying is Chinese and everybody believe them. Traditional orange chicken (chen pi ji) is Hunan, made with chicken and dried citrus peel like tangerine, orange, and lemon. Orange chicken like one at P.F. Chang's is deep-fry and coated in orange juice sauce and a lot of sugar. (Sweet and cheap, how Uncle Roger like it.) Uncle Roger good friend DimSimLim (Vincent Lim aka @wokgod) make best version of fast-food orange chicken. Uncle DimSimLim like to eat orange chicken with noodles, Uncle Roger like steam or Egg Fry Rice (page 38). You choose. Uncle Roger *promise* this nothing like Rachael Ray orange chicken.

Neutral oil, for deep-frying

Finely ground white pepper

MSG, King of Flavor

MARINATED CHICKEN

About 1¼ pounds boneless, skinless chicken thighs

1 tablespoon cornstarch

2 teaspoons chicken bouillon powder *(Very smart, this have both salt and MSG.)*

½-inch piece finely chopped ginger (about 1½ teaspoons)

1 tablespoon sesame oil

2 teaspoons Shaoxing rice wine

BATTER

½ cup cornstarch *(This very good Asian recipe. It keep listing same ingredient like cornstarch again in each section. This so you don't get confused on amount each time you add it.)*

1 cup self-rising flour, or 1 cup all-purpose flour plus 1½ teaspoons baking powder

ORANGE SAUCE

1 cup store-bought orange juice

1 tablespoon cornstarch *(potato starch that Uncle DimSimLim use make sauce silkier, but cornstarch also do good job.)*

3 tablespoons Thai sweet chilli sauce

2 tablespoons unseasoned rice vinegar

1 tablespoon soy sauce

2 tablespoons granulated sugar

3 garlic cloves, finely chopped

½-inch piece finely chopped ginger *(about 1½ teaspoons)*

1 to 1½ small dried red chillies, like Thai jindas or chiles de árbol, chopped, or 1 teaspoon chilli flakes

TO SERVE

1 to 2 spoonfuls (about 1½ tablespoons) sesame seeds, lightly toasted

1 scallion, sliced *(Green part only, now garnish count as vegetable.)*

Steamed or fried rice, or noodles

Recipe continues

AUNTIE ESTHER'S CHICKEN KATSU CURRY RAMEN

SERVES 2 *(Uncle Roger and Auntie Esther . . .)*

Remember when Uncle Roger fly all the way to New York to meet Auntie Esther at her New York restaurant Mŏkbar? She make Uncle Roger this version of Japanese katsu stuffed with cheese and serve it on her curry ramen with pretty pink drink. So romantic.

Neutral oil, for deep-frying

Fine table salt

MSG, King of Flavor *(Auntie Esther LOVE MSG. That is why she the Queen of Flavor.)*

CHICKEN ROLLS

2 large bone-in, skin-on chicken thighs (6 to 7 ounces each)

4 ounces block *(not fresh!)* mozzarella

VEGETABLE CURRY

4 tablespoons unsalted butter

½ medium yellow onion, chopped

2 to 3 medium carrots, peeled and cut into bite-size pieces

3 garlic cloves, minced

1-inch piece finely chopped ginger (about 1 tablespoon)

2 tablespoons all-purpose flour

2 tablespoons Uncle Roger's Spicy-Hot Curry Powder (recipe follows)

3½ to 4 cups chicken broth *(Chefs make stock with chicken thigh bone, Uncle Roger just buy broth or rehydrate bouillon.)*

A handful (about ⅓ cup) of shelled fresh peas, if in season *(Why so many vegetable, haiyaa . . .)*

Chilli powder, for seasoning *(Your favorite chilli powder, this just to adjust spice.)*

FRIED CHICKEN

¼ cup all-purpose flour

Generous ½ cup panko bread crumbs

1 egg, beaten with chopsticks

TO SERVE

8 to 10 ounces fresh ramen noodles *(Uncle Roger like thinner noodle for this, not too thick.)*

Sesame seeds, lightly toasted, for sprinkling

1 scallion, lighter green stalk sliced into long, thin strips *(Make it pretty, like Auntie Esther.)*

About ½ long (pinky-length) red Thai chilli, sliced *(Another pretty little garnish of chilli just for a pop of red color, so New York fancy. No Asian home cook would waste time with this.)*

Recipe continues

CHICKEN ROLLS

Cut out the chicken bones *(kitchen scissor make it easy)* and remove the skin. Pound the chicken thighs with the flat side of a meat mallet, rolling pin, or heavy pan to roughly the size of your hand (4 by 6 inches) and about ¼ inch thick. *(Auntie Esther so violent.)* Season the chicken lightly with 3 to 4 pinches of both salt and MSG. *(Auntie Esther must have forgotten this step because not in weejio. She too nervous flirting with Uncle Roger.)*

Slice the mozzarella into 2 rectangular slabs, each about 1½ × 3 inches and ½ inch thick. Lay 1 slice of mozzarella at the widest end of each chicken thigh. Trim the edges of the cheese so it fits within the thigh; each block shouldn't be more than one-third the size of the chicken thigh. *(Size of mozzarella depend on how big each chicken thigh. If too big, can't roll up chicken. If too small, not enough cheese oozes out when cut open chicken roll after frying.)* Tightly roll up the meat and wrap in plastic wrap, twisting the plastic wrap like a candy wrapper to snugly enclose each chicken roll. *(Must have very tight roll. Loose roll fall apart when fry, haiyaa.)* Refrigerate the chicken rolls for at least 2 hours or up to overnight.

VEGETABLE CURRY

In a large saucepan, melt the butter over medium-high heat. Add the onion and sauté, stirring occasionally, until golden brown, 8 to 10 minutes. *(Auntie Esther use big French word, sauté, and she cook in skillet, not wok. Ancestor crying.)*

Add the carrots, garlic, and ginger and sauté until aromatic, about 2 minutes. While whisking, add the flour and curry powder and whisk constantly until the roux smells toasty and darkens somewhat, about 2 minutes, then slowly pour about ½ cup chicken broth into the skillet. Scrape the browned bits off the bottom of the pan, add another 3 cups chicken broth and 5 to 6 pinches of MSG, and gently boil the sauce, stirring occasionally, for about 10 minutes.

Add the peas and cook until the carrots and peas are tender, another 8 to 10 minutes. The curry should coat a spoon; if the sauce thickens into more of a gravy, thin it with a little chicken broth. Adjust the seasonings with chilli powder or salt; the curry should be well seasoned.

FRIED CHICKEN

When ready to fry the chicken, put a rack over a baking sheet. *(Just lay rack on whatever you have near the stove—a pot, a plate.)* Fill a wok or medium saucepot with tall sides (big enough to submerge 1 or 2 chicken rolls) with enough oil to completely submerge the chicken. Heat the oil until very hot, about 350°F (175°C); the oil should be shimmering. *(Only Western people use thermometer, use feeling!)*

Put the flour and panko in separate piles and the eggs in a bowl. Dredge each chicken roll in the flour, dunk in the eggs and shake off the excess liquid, then roll in the panko. Press the panko firmly onto the surface of the rolls with your hands so it adheres. *(Give roll gentle little squeeze.)*

Deep-fry the chicken rolls until dark golden brown and a digital thermometer reads 160°F (about 70°C) or the chicken rolls are very firm to the touch, about 10 minutes. *(Big chicken roll is so girthy, cook longer than smaller roll. If unsure, better to cook longer because nobody like salmonella.)* Transfer the chicken to the rack and season with salt while hot.

Meanwhile, fill a sauce pot with enough water to generously cover the ramen and bring to a boil.

(Are you ready to eat? Noodle don't wait.)

TO SERVE

When the chicken is almost ready, boil thin ramen noodles for about 1 minute and medium-thick noodles for 2 to 3 minutes. *(Use feeling, cook till noodle at firmness you like.)* Scoop out the noodles, add about three-quarters to the vegetable curry, and stir and toss the ramen until well coated in curry sauce. Add more noodles, if you'd like; the curry should be fairly brothy.

Divide the ramen noodles between two serving bowls and sprinkle the sesame seeds on top. Lay the chicken rolls flat on a work surface so the block of cheese inside is lying flat, like a deck of cards. Slice the rolls in half lengthwise, through the middle, and open up the halves like a book. Lay the chicken halves on top of the noodles. *(If you f—k up and slice the katsu the wrong way, all that sexy cheese won't ooze out. Just spread out the cheese over the surface or sprinkle a little more cheese on top like you are making a potato skin. Blast it under broiler until it get melty. Problem solved. Uncle Roger should be big New York chef.)*

Top the chicken katsu with the strips of scallion and a few red chilli slices. *(Put on romantic Jacky Cheung song and enjoy with your loved one.)*

✗ HAIYAA . . .

Most flimsy boneless chicken thigh sold at Western grocery store fall apart when do so much pounding. And too small to hold a nice, thick slice of cheese. Buy big bone-in thighs and cut out bone, now have perfect katsu chicken. (Make stock with bone and vegetable scraps.)

✓ FUIYOH!

Fresh ramen noodle always best!

You can pound, stuff, and fry the chicken, and even make curry sauce ahead. When your date arrive, reheat chicken and curry. (Rewarm chicken roll on a rack in 325°F/160°C oven until hot and the cheese nice and melty, 10 to 15 minutes.) Boil noodle, ready for date.

UNCLE ROGER'S SPICY-HOT CURRY POWDER

Auntie Esther make Uncle Roger pound 14 spices for 3 hour to make her spicy curry powder! That way too much pounding, even for Uncle Roger. I add a few spices that Auntie Esther likes to the spicy Malaysian meat curry powder that my mum use in her Malaysian Chicken Curry (page 134). Work perfect, and so easy. That meat curry powder also in my Malaysian Fried Chicken (page 204) and other recipes in my book. Worth it to get a bag.

Makes about 2 tablespoons

¼ teaspoon fenugreek seeds

¼ teaspoon black mustard seeds

2 tablespoons Malaysian meat curry powder, like Baba's or Alagappa's

In a mortar, pound the fenugreek and black mustard seeds to a coarse powder, then mix in the curry powder.

▶ Weejios

Uncle Roger Meet His Favorite Chef (with @ChoiBites)

Last Chance to Impress Auntie Esther (with @ChoiBites)

DISPOSABLE
HYGIENIC

UNCLE ROGER'S TAKEOUT-STYLE EGG ROLLS

MAKES 8 EGG ROLLS

Western-style egg roll are one of Chinese people greatest gift to America. Ancestor add egg to spring roll wrapper so it get extra crispy when fried and fill it with whatever strip-mall cook have in back of refrigerator—shredded cabbage, carrot, maybe some mushroom, leftover chicken or pork, and at fancy places, sometimes shrimp. Uncle Roger make mine with chicken thigh so filling isn't too wet, include some aromatics I like (galangal, FUIYOH!) and a splash of Shaoxing rice wine for a special touch.

Neutral oil, for stir-frying

MSG, King of Flavor

FILLING

8 ounces boneless, skinless chicken thighs (2 medium)

1 tablespoon plus 2 teaspoons soy sauce

About ⅓ medium head Chinese (napa) cabbage, sliced in half lengthwise

1 large thick carrot, peeled

2 ounces (1 cup) beech or other small mushrooms

2 garlic cloves, finely chopped

2-inch piece finely chopped galangal (about 2 tablespoons)

½-inch piece finely chopped ginger (about 1½ teaspoons)

1 tablespoon Shaoxing rice wine

½ teaspoon granulated sugar

3 scallions, chopped *(For egg roll you want both white bulb and lighter green part, no dark green ends.)*

ASSEMBLY AND FRYING

8 egg roll wrappers (about ½ a 1-pound package), thawed *(Western grocery store brand like Dynasty work best. Most Chinese brand that say egg roll really for spring roll.)*

TO SERVE

Any sauce you like: *(Panda Express have all FIVE sauce choices for one little egg roll. USA really is land of the free when it come to condiment. Uncle Roger like Thai chilli sauce for little bit of sweetness.)*

Thai sweet chilli sauce, sweet and sour sauce, Chinese hot mustard, teriyaki sauce, or soy sauce

Recipe continues

FILLING *(Sometime Uncle Roger make filling in the morning, refrigerate until hungry later. Leave filling in bowl with paper towel to soak up any extra juices that make egg roll soggy.)*

Line a bowl with paper towels. Cut each chicken thigh into 3 or 4 pieces.

In a wok or small saucepan, combine the chicken thighs, 1 tablespoon of the soy sauce, and 3 tablespoons water. Bring to a gentle boil and cook just until the chicken is no longer pink, about 5 minutes. Take the pot off the heat and let the chicken cool for about 5 minutes. Drain, shred into bite-size pieces, and season generously with MSG. *(Don't skimp on MSG! Chicken need good flavor.)*

Thinly slice the finer cabbage fronds. Slice, then chop the crunchier bottom stems. *(Want about 4 cups, a good mix of soft tops and crunchy bottom leaves.)* Grate the carrot on the large holes of a box grater. Chop the mushrooms.

Heat a wok until hot. Add about 2 tablespoons oil and swirl to evenly coat the surface. Reduce the heat to medium and stir-fry the garlic, galangal, and ginger for a few seconds. Add the cabbage, carrot, and mushrooms and toss and stir-fry until the vegetables just begin to wilt, about 1½ minutes. Add the rice wine, remaining 2 teaspoons soy sauce, and sugar and stir until the liquid is mostly absorbed, about 30 seconds. Turn off the heat, add the scallions and chicken, and toss to combine. Adjust the seasonings with soy sauce or MSG. Scrape the filling into the paper towel–lined bowl.

ASSEMBLY AND FRYING *(Don't assemble egg roll before ready to fry or filling will make wrappers soggy, haiyaa . . .)*

Set a baking rack or sheet pan (to drain egg rolls) over a pot and set aside a small dish of water.

Lay 1 egg roll wrapper with 1 corner facing downward to make a diamond shape. *(If you messed up and bought thinner spring roll wrapper from Asian market, use 2 wrappers.)* Put a handful (about ⅓ cup packed) of filling about 3 inches from the bottom corner of the wrapper and shape the filling into a compact log about 4 inches long. Lift up the bottom corner of the wrapper to cover the filling, then fold in both sides to enclose the filling like you're making a burrito. *(Want nice tight roll, everything firmly packed inside.)* With your finger, lightly brush the top corner of the wrapper with water, then finish rolling up the egg roll and lay it seam side facing down. If your hands are damp, dry them off before assembling the remaining egg rolls.

When ready to fry, line a baking rack with paper towels. *(Don't even think about using air fryer. Egg roll won't get a nice crust. Uncle Roger only approve of reheating your frozen deep-fried egg rolls in air fryer.)*

In a wok, heat 2 to 3 finger joints (2 to 3 inches) oil until very hot, 350° to 360°F (about 180°C). *(Do chopstick test!)*

Fry the egg rolls, no more than 4 at a time, until golden brown, about 5 minutes; flip the egg rolls a few times as they fry to brown both sides. *(Egg roll float so need to flip.)* Shake off the excess oil and transfer the egg rolls to the baking rack. Reheat the oil before frying each batch of egg rolls or the skin won't crisp up.

TO SERVE

Let the egg rolls cool for about 10 minutes and serve with your favorite dipping sauce. *(Egg roll VERY hot when it come right out of fryer. Be careful, but don't let it cool too much. Egg roll lose crispiness the longer they sit.)* If frying the egg rolls a few hours before serving, you can rewarm them on the baking rack (remove the paper towels) in a preheated 350°F (180°C) oven until hot. *(Squeeze egg roll to see if hot, 5 minute, 8 minute, not too long. Use feeling.)*

Once fried, any leftover egg rolls will become soggy if refrigerated but can be frozen. Reheat the frozen egg rolls (don't thaw) in a preheated 375°F (190°C) air-fryer for about 10 minutes. *(Air fryer work best, stay crispiest because circulate hot air, but too expensive for Uncle Roger. I use my regular oven heated to the same temperature. Put egg roll on rack, bake for about 15 minute, flip egg rolls once. Perfect late-night snack.)*

× HAIYAA . . .

If no egg in wrapper, it not egg roll! Egg roll wrapper like Dynasty brand at Western grocery store very important for crinkly, extra-crispy texture and nice golden-brown color. (It more like wonton wrapper, very sturdy so can hold all egg roll ingredient.) True Chinese spring roll wrapper in freezer section of many Asian grocery store is thinner and don't get nice bubbly skin when fry, stays smooth (because no egg in wrapper).

This not coleslaw. Uncle Roger don't want to see my recipe improvised with bagged coleslaw mix. Insulting to Asian people everywhere. Chinese cabbage is best for different textures. Get nice mix of delicate, frilly top leaves and crunchy bottom leaves.

CAJUN FRY RICE

SERVES 1 CHEF RUSH, OR 2 TO 3 NORMAL-SIZE PEOPLE

After all the auntie in Uncle Roger life leave me, Uncle Roger needed help from an expert with the ladies: Chef Andrew Rush, former White House chef with muscles bigger than America defense budget. Uncle Roger even went to gym to get a training session from the master. After Chef Rush pound Uncle Roger in workout, he make his special Cajun version of fry rice. It has that perfect Blasian flavor. This is NOT authentic fry rice like my recipes (they start on page 37). That OK. Chef Rush can kill Uncle Roger with one punch so he get to make fry rice however he want.

Chef Rush make his fry rice extra high in protein, with both sausage and shrimp to build big muscles, and include one of Uncle Roger favorite nonvegetables: okra. (Before you knock it, okra is actually interesting in fry rice.) But the real secret to this fry rice is it combine Asian people MSG (the cocaine of cooking, FUIYOH!) with Black people MSG, Creole seasoning. (There is no white people MSG. Do you know why? They hate flavor.) There is only one small problem with this recipe. Chef Rush fry rice was supposed to get me a new auntie. Still waiting.

Unsalted butter and neutral oil, for stir-frying *(butter so American . . .)*

Finely ground white pepper

MSG, King of Flavor

About 12 ounces andouille sausage

About 12 ounces shrimp (14 to 16 medium), peeled and deveined, or crawfish tails *(Chef Rush live in Los Angeles where can't get crawfish. Chinese people call them xiaolongxia 小龙虾.)*

About ½ teaspoon Tony Chachere's Creole Seasoning, plus more for seasoning the shrimp

3 tablespoons finely chopped white or yellow onion

6 to 8 okra pods, thickly sliced *(fresh not mushy frozen okra, haiyaa)*

A handful (about ½ cup) of corn kernels *(Uncle Roger like fresh but frozen OK.)*

½ small celery stalk, sliced *(Why so many vegetable?)*

½ medium red or green bell pepper, chopped *(Chef Rush like sweet red pepper. Green pepper is traditional, more savory flavor. You choose.)*

2 eggs

3 Asian-size bowls (about 3 cups) day-old rice, broken up with your fingers *(day or two old, sat in fridge)*

About 2½ tablespoons soy sauce *(Creole seasoning is very salty, so Uncle Roger use less soy sauce.)*

2 scallions, sliced *(Green part only!)*

1 to 2 Thai bird's eye chillies, diced, or 2 long (pinky-length) red or green Thai chillies, sliced

Recipe continues

Slice the sausage into thick bite-size pieces. Season the shrimp lightly with Creole seasoning. *(Pretend you are using table salt when you season shrimp. Tony Cachere seasoning very salty.)*

Heat a wok until hot. Add about 2 tablespoons butter and swirl to evenly coat the surface. *(Wok does not need to be seasoned because it should be less hot than normal fry rice. Butter can burn.)* Spread out the sausage in a single layer, sear for about 10 seconds. Add the shrimp and toss and stir-fry just until the shrimp is no longer translucent, about 1 minute. Scrape into a bowl. *(Mmmm . . . smell so good.)*

Reheat the wok, add about 1½ tablespoons oil, and heat again. *(Crank up the heat, now get wok nice and hot.)* Add the onion and okra and stir-fry for about 30 seconds. Add the corn, celery, and bell pepper and toss and stir-fry until the vegetables just begin to soften on the edges, about 30 seconds. *(Uncle Roger can't bench press like Chef Rush but I can toss.)*

Add the eggs and break them up with the wok turner only until very loosely set. *(Like when you make Uncle Roger fry rice, now you bang, bang, bang constantly on the bottom of the wok. If fry eggs more than a few seconds, they overcook.)* Add the rice and spread it out with the wok turner so it doesn't clump together. Sprinkle about ½ teaspoon Creole seasoning *(use feeling!)*, 2 to 3 pinches of white pepper, and 1 BIG pinch of MSG over the rice and stir a few times. Add the soy sauce and toss and stir until the rice darkens from the soy sauce, then add the sausage and shrimp. Toss and stir a few more times and adjust the seasoning with soy sauce or Creole seasoning.

Scatter the scallion greens and chillies over the rice and keep tossing and stirring until no clumps of rice remain. *(Hard to get proper "jumping" grain of rice because this such a big quantity of fry rice. That OK.)* Scrape the fried rice onto a plate. *(Eat! Chef Rush does not wait.)*

Weejio

Uncle Roger Train to Get Auntie (with @ChefRush)

FORTUNE COOKIES

MAKES 10 TO 11 COOKIES

A fortune cookie is one of Uncle Roger favorite things about Chinese takeout. Little something sweet and crispy to end the meal that come with a surprise inside. The best thing about fortune cookie is the false hope it give you. One time Uncle Roger got this fortune: "An old acquaintance will re-enter your life." But Auntie Esther never call.

The factories that make fortune cookies for all the thousands of Chinese take-out places have special machine that spread out the batter into very thin circle. When each cookie is baked, the machine quickly inserts a fortune and shapes the perfect cookie before it gets too hard to bend. (This is very good analogy for life. Always go with young cookies. Old ones too stubborn and stiff.) Shaping the cookie is a little harder at home, but Uncle Roger have confidence in you.

- Butter, neutral oil, or cooking spray, for the baking sheets
- Fine table salt
- ¼ cup egg whites from 2 large eggs *(or cheap liquid egg white)*
- ½ cup granulated sugar
- 2 tablespoons neutral oil
- ¼ teaspoon vanilla extract
- ¼ teaspoon almond extract
- ½ cup all-purpose flour
- 1½ teaspoons cornstarch
- About 1½ tablespoons sesame seeds (optional), for sprinkling
- 10 to 11 fortune papers *(Cut out thin strip of paper about 2 finger joints long, write fortune on each.)*

Preheat the oven to 325°F (160°C) and put a rack in the middle of the oven. Butter or spray a nonstick baking sheet. *(Use a LOT of butter or cooking spray on baking sheet, keep cookie from sticking. If have a fancy baking mat, that also works, but NO parchment paper, cookie get crinkly, haiyaa.)* Have a muffin tin and thick-rimmed coffee mug nearby.

In a medium bowl, vigorously whisk together the egg whites and sugar for about 45 seconds; the eggs will have bubbles on the surface. Add the oil, vanilla, almond extract, and 1 tablespoon water and mix just to combine. Whisk in the flour, cornstarch, and 2 pinches of salt until fairly smooth; a few lumps are fine.

Put 1 tablespoon of batter in the center of the baking sheet. *(Scrape out ALL of the batter in the measuring spoon!)* Move your finger in a circular motion to gently spread out the batter into a round 3 to 3½ inches wide. Shape 4 more cookies into rounds, leaving plenty of room between them. Once the batter has settled, go

Recipe continues

An old acquaintance
will re-enter your life.

back and spread out each cookie into roughly a 4-inch round. *(Pull out your ruler. Must get batter thin enough or fortune cookie too thick to get crispy.)* If you'd like, sprinkle sesame seeds just around the edges of each cookie. *(Very fancy, Uncle Roger like sesame seeds. It will impress the aunties.)*

Bake the cookies just until the very edges of each cookie are lightly browned, 11 to 14 minutes, rotating the pan front to back halfway through. *(Check early! Every oven have different bake time. Bake too long and cookies will stick to baking sheet and break. Not long enough and won't crisp up.)*

Working quickly, run the knife under one side of each cookie to help lift up the edge, then use a spatula to flip each cookie upside down. Lay 1 fortune paper near the center of each cookie. *(Stop looking at your phone! Must hurry.)*

Quickly fold 1 cookie in half and pick it up like a taco, seam side facing up. *(Yes, cookie is hot. Just learn to deal with hot thing, don't be weak.)* Lay the center of the cookie on the rim of the mug and gently pull down on the bottom edges to shape the 2 lobes of the fortune cookie. Lay the cookie on its side in the muffin tin, closing any large gaps in the seam as you do. *(Cookie always want to pop back open and become a taco again. Muffin tin force cookie to retain its shape as it cools.)* As you shape the remaining cookies, if any are too cool to shape, put the baking sheet back in the oven for about 15 seconds before shaping the cookies. *(Making fortune cookie is harder than Uncle Roger thought. Should have just ordered takeout and gotten free cookies.)*

Scrape any cookie crumbs off the baking sheet and reapply butter, oil, or spray before baking the remaining cookies. *(Don't wait! If batter sit too long it stiffen up, like Uncle Roger.)*

The cookies are best eaten the same day but will keep for about 3 days in a tightly sealed food storage bag. Press the air out of the bag and add a small piece of paper towel to help retain the crispy texture.

✓ FUIYOH!

Egg so expensive when Uncle Roger was working on recipes for this book. I buy liquid egg white, cheap and easy. No mess.

Recipe No
Tracklements
fresh
chilli jam

THE WORST RECIPES IN THIS BOOK

HAIYAA, WHY ARE YOU EVEN READING THIS CHAPTER? TRUST UNCLE ROGER. SKIP THESE PAGES. GO TO NEXT CHAPTER (PAGE 125) WITH RECIPES FROM UNCLE ROGER FAVORITE AUNTIE OF ALL TIME.

CHILLI JAM

(aka Uncle Roger's least favorite recipe in this book)

MAKES 1 SMALL JAR (ABOUT ½ CUP)

The day Jamie Oliver use chilli jam in his egg fry rice was day Uncle Roger discover the horrors of British fry rice. They say keep your friend close but keep your enemy closer. Uncle Roger go all the way to chilli jam factory, Tracklements, 100 mile south of London, to find out what in this jam Jamie Oliver like so much.

Nephew Guy Tullberg who own Tracklements say company make 15,000 jar a day. (All go to Jamie Oliver restaurants.) Jamie Oliver even make his own homemade version of Nephew Guy's jam in a weejio, and he even screw up that recipe. (Just buy jar of Tracklements, haiyaa. It say every ingredient on label.) Nephew Guy say he get idea for chilli jam when he go on vacation to Thailand. (Who bring back recipe from Asia? Supposed to bring back woman.) Nephew Guy must have gotten recipe at overprice tourist shop because Tracklements chilli jam not spicy. It missing key Thai chilli jam ingredient: fish sauce, tamarind, dried shrimp, spicy dried chillies. (Buy a jar for yourself, see what you think.) That OK, Uncle Roger like Nephew Guy. He let Uncle Roger make chilli jam at factory and stir his big pot.

Fine table salt

2 small dried red chillies, like Thai jindas or chiles de árbol

½ cup finely chopped red bell pepper (about ½ large)

1 tablespoon finely chopped shallots or red onions *(How Jamie Oliver forget onion? Say onion right on jar.)*

1 small garlic clove, finely chopped

⅔ cup loosely packed dark brown sugar

2½ tablespoons raw unfiltered apple cider vinegar

2 teaspoons powdered pectin

Soften the small dried chillies in hot water for about 10 minutes. *(Scrape out seeds, Jamie Oliver can't handle any spice.)*

In a deep medium saucepan, combine the chillies, bell pepper, shallots, garlic, sugar, vinegar, 2 pinches of salt, and ¾ cup water and bring to a vigorous boil over high heat. Reduce the heat to medium and boil for 15 minutes.

In a small dish, stir together the pectin and 2 tablespoons water with your fingers until completely smooth. Remove the saucepan from heat and very quickly whisk in the pectin so it does not form clumps. *(If it does, who care? This chilli jam.)* Return to a vigorous boil and boil for 2 minutes, then remove from the heat. *(Boil hard to set pectin.)* The jam will have more of a

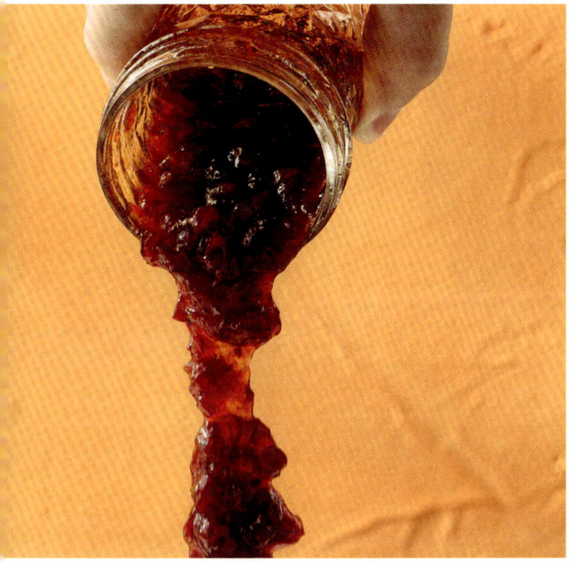

Weejios

Uncle Roger Visit Chilli Jam Factory (with @Tracklements)

Uncle Roger HATE Jamie Oliver Egg Fried Rice

Homemade Chilli Jam *(This Jamie Oliver recipe version. Go to @JamieOliver YouTube page for weejio, if you dare.)*

syrup consistency at this point but will thicken up as it cools. Let the jam cool in the saucepan, then cover and refrigerate overnight; after 24 hours it will have thickened but will still be more loosely set than many jams.

Refrigerate the jam for up to 2 months.

✔ FUIYOH!

Remember, chilli jam on its own is not a good, but also not a bad, ingredient. It how you use it. And Jamie definitely abuse it. In that egg fry rice weejio, chilli jam is victim also. Chilli jam best with cracker and cheese. Uncle Guy make nice spread for Uncle Roger: layer of cream cheese, chilli jam, and a little cilantro on top. NO CHILLI JAM ON FRY RICE!

Good Morning

GRILLED CHEESE

(better than Gordon Ramsay grill cheese but still a sad, Western sandwich with no flavor)

MAKES 1 UNCLE ROGER–APPROVED GRILLED CHEESE

Grilled cheese easiest thing to make, only two ingredient: Grill and Cheese. Uncle Gordon f—k up whole thing. Use wrong stove. (Nobody cook grill cheese in fireplace!) Wrong bread. (Thick sourdough bread with hard, dry crust cut your mouth and take too long to toast, haiyaa.) Wrong cheese. (Romano with pepperberry and Asiago too dry. Not going to melt! And what the hell is pepperberry?) AND he use kimchi. (WHAT?! Niece and nephew, Uncle Roger have to put leg down from chair.) Gordon say kimchi add acid. Nobody eating grilled cheese and thinking this sandwich not corrosive enough, need more acid.

Niece and nephew, THIS is how you make a Western grilled cheese.

- MSG, King of Flavor
- Plenty of butter, at room temperature
- 2 slices plain white sandwich bread, like Wonder
- 2 to 3 slices American cheese *(Kraft Singles or cheap generic brand, all taste same)*

Butter the bread generously on both sides. *(Gordon Ramsay pour whole bottle of olive oil in iron skillet, haiyaa.)*

Heat a skillet over medium heat. *(Not too hot! This not fry rice. Cook over low heat or bread burn.)* Lightly toast the bread on one side, then flip the slices. *(This step warm up bread, help cheese melt, and bread stay just a little crunchy.)*

Lay 2 or 3 slices American cheese on 1 slice of bread and sprinkle 1 BIG pinch of MSG on top. *(FUIYOH! Uncle Roger little Asian treat for Americans.)* Close the sandwich and cook the grilled cheese until the bread is lightly toasted on both sides and the cheese has melted. *(Don't push down on bread while it cook, haiyaa. Lose all that good melted cheese. If have to push down on bread, your sandwich too thick and the fire too far from cheese, not going to reach sandwich. Fire and cheese in long distance relationship. How that going to work?)*

Transfer the grilled cheese to a plate. *(Eat while you watch weejio of Nephew Gordon make worse grill cheese ever. He lost his uncle status from this grilled cheese weejio, but don't worry, he regain it back when we make bao together.)*

Weejios

Gordon Ramsay Messed Up the Simplest Dish (Grilled Cheese)

Can Gordon Ramsay Get His Uncle Crown Back from Uncle Roger?? (via @GordonRamsay)

UNCLE ROGER FAVORITE RECIPES IN WHOLE WORLD

(FROM MY MUM!)

UNCLE ROGER HEART RATE STILL ELEVATED AFTER THAT LAST CHAPTER (PAGE 119), HAIYAA. RECOVERING WITH AUTHENTIC, DELICIOUS ASIAN FOOD IN THIS CHAPTER. ALL ARE THINGS I EAT AS A KID GROWING UP. BRING BACK GOOD MEMORY. BEFORE I DISCOVER JAMIE OLIVER.

SARAWAK ACAR

(Sweet and Sour Pickled Cucumber)

MAKES 5 TO 6 CUPS

Acar is spicy-sweet, pickled vegetable that Southeast Asian people eat as side dish or scoop up with keropok. It like Malaysian version of kimchi. Every auntie have her own recipe. This one is Uncle Roger favorite. My mum make hers nice and spicy. FUIYOH!

Very important that all vegetable are same size. Need to cut cucumber and carrots into thin matchstick. When too thick, it too hard to squeeze out all the water. Drying cucumber and carrot under sun for two to three hours make them extra crunchy and crispy. Fresh chilli paste for gravy should be very spicy. I use Thailand chilli, not bird's eye. —Uncle Roger Mum

Neutral oil, for frying

Fine table salt

SAUCE

⅓ cup long (pinky-length) red or green Thai chillies, sliced

2 to 3 small Asian or 1 medium Western shallot, diced

1 stalk lemongrass, peeled, ends trimmed, and tender bottom half sliced

3-inch piece roughly chopped or shaved galangal (about 3 tablespoons)

2-inch piece roughly chopped turmeric (about 2 tablespoons)

⅔ cup unseasoned rice vinegar

1½ cups granulated sugar

VEGETABLES

About 2 pounds large thick cucumbers *(Don't peel cucumber! Need about 3, depending on size. Nobody weigh.)*

About 12 ounces large thick carrots, peeled *(Nothing puny, need 2 to 3 jumbo carrots to cut into matchstick.)*

TO FINISH

4-inch piece finely chopped ginger (about 4 tablespoons)

4 to 5 garlic cloves, finely chopped

2 to 3 spoonfuls (2 to 3 tablespoons) white sesame seeds, or more if you want

TO SERVE

Keropok

(Sarawak acar also go with so many dishes, Uncle Roger even spoon it up for a snack.)

SAUCE

In a large mortar, pound the chillies to a coarse paste. Add the shallots, lemongrass, galangal, turmeric, and 2 spoonfuls (about 2 tablespoons) water and grind to a paste. *(Or blitz everything in a spice or coffee grinder that can handle wet ingredient. Even Uncle Roger mum get tired.)*

Heat a wok until hot. Add about 2 tablespoons oil and swirl to evenly coat the surface. *(Oil should not be smoking, this not fry rice.)* Reduce the heat to medium, add the spice paste and cook, stirring regularly, until thick, 8 to 10 minutes.

Recipe continues

绍兴料酒

FRIED PORK BELLY

Put the pork belly in a medium bowl. Make a space off to one side of the bowl and mash together 1 square bean curd, egg, 1 teaspoon oyster sauce, cornstarch, ½ teaspoon sugar, ½ teaspoon five-spice powder, ½ teaspoon white pepper, and 2 to 3 pinches of salt. Coat the pork belly in the marinade and refrigerate for at least 4 hours or overnight. *(Overnight best, intensify flavor.)*

To fry the pork belly, line a large plate with paper towels. *(Pork belly so fatty, paper towel drain off more of fat. If you cheap like Uncle Roger, drain on rack.)*

Fill a wok with at least 2 finger joints (2 inches) oil and heat until very hot; it should be shimmering.

Stir the pork to lightly recoat all the pieces in the marinade. In batches, deep-fry the pork belly, flipping the pieces occasionally, until golden brown, 6 to 8 minutes. *(Want nice color.)* Transfer the pork belly to the paper towels.

BRAISING SAUCE

Tear the black fungus into large bite-size pieces; discard any thicker woody bits.

In a wok with a lid or pot, heat about 2 tablespoons oil over medium-high heat. Add the garlic and fry a few seconds until aromatic, then add the black fungus and stir-fry until softened, about 1 minute. Add the fried pork belly and enough water to cover the meat by 1 finger joint (about 4 cups). Smash the remaining 2 squares bean curd and add them to the pot with 1 tablespoon oyster sauce, soy sauce, rice wine, 1 teaspoon sugar, ½ teaspoon Chinese five-spice powder, star anise, and 1½ teaspoons white pepper and bring to a gentle boil. Cover the pot, and cook, stirring occasionally, until the pork is tender, about 45 minutes. Adjust the seasonings with sugar or salt.

TO SERVE

Scatter the cilantro over the pork belly and serve with the steamed rice.

× HAIYAA . . .

Uncle Roger never find pork belly at Western "grocery store," only at expensive butcher shop. Say grocery store on sign and place doesn't even sell world's best and cheapest cut of pork? That false advertising. At Asian market, you can get all different cuts, like boneless pork belly with skin that already cut up into perfect little pieces for recipe. AND it have plenty of fat. Don't get ones with too much meat, too tough, hard to chew.

FERMENTED RED BEAN CURD

Little squares of tofu fermented and aged in red yeast sauce for umami flavor called hongfuru or nam yu; some Western people call it soy cheese. Longer bean curd is aged, the more expensive it is. No reason to waste money with this recipe, so many other big flavor. Basic jar like HT or Wangzhihe very good.

MY MUM'S CHICKEN CURRY! MMMM.
GET RECIPE ON THE NEXT PAGE.

MALAYSIAN CHICKEN CURRY

(Kari Ayam)

SERVES 5 OR 6

This Uncle Roger favorite chicken curry. Malaysian chicken curry not like Indian curry, supposed to have a LOT of sauce. More watery like soup. Must use the right curry powder! Malaysian curry powder is spicy, not like any other.

Amount of potato depend on your preference. You want chicken to have very soft texture and be coated in santan (coconut cream) gravy. Serve chicken curry with steam rice, noodle, or roti canai. —Uncle Roger Mum

Neutral oil, for frying

Fine table salt

About 4½ tablespoons Malaysian meat curry powder, like Baba's or Alagappa's, divided

About 1½ pounds bone-in, skin-on chicken thighs or a mix of thighs and drumsticks *(need enough so everybody get 1 whole piece of chicken)*

3 long (pinky-length) red or green Thai chillies, seeds removed and sliced

1 Thai bird's eye chilli, seeds removed and sliced, or another long Thai chilli

8 to 9 small Asian or 3 medium Western shallots, roughly chopped

3 stalks lemongrass: 1 stalk peeled, trimmed, and sliced, and 2 stalks smashed

3 to 4 garlic cloves, smashed

3 to 4 medium yellow or red potatoes, peeled and cut into bite-size pieces

6 to 8 fresh or frozen curry leaves *(Dried leaf only if no other option but don't fry those.)*

½ cup thick coconut cream *(Called santan, read Uncle Roger note if you don't know what this is.)*

About 2 teaspoons granulated sugar

TO SERVE

Steamed rice, noodles, or roti canai (or other flatbread)

Rub a generous spoonful (about 1½ tablespoons) curry powder all over the chicken and refrigerate for at least 30 minutes or up to 6 hours. *(Don't waste plastic wrap to cover bowl, haiyaa. Throw in refrigerator.)*

In a mortar, pound both chillies until coarsely ground. Add the shallots, 1 stalk sliced lemongrass, garlic, and 2 spoonfuls (about 2 tablespoons) water and pound to a coarse paste. *(If lazy, grind all ingredient in a blender but need to smash up chillies first into small pieces.)*

Heat a wok with a lid or a pot until hot. Add about 2 tablespoons oil and swirl to evenly coat the surface. Stir-fry the potatoes until golden brown and scrape onto a plate; the potatoes will finish cooking in the curry. *(Get two sides of potato nice and brown, that enough. Uncle Roger hungry.)*

Add another 2 tablespoons oil to the wok and reduce the heat to medium. Add the chilli paste and cook, stirring regularly, until the paste thickens and the oil separates, about 10 minutes.

Clear out a space in the center of the wok, add another splash of oil, and fry the curry leaves for a few seconds. *(Don't fry if using dried leaf. Add later.)* Add 3 spoonfuls (about 3 tablespoons) curry powder and stir for a few seconds, then add a generous splash of water and scrape the spices off the bottom of the wok. *(Amount of water doesn't matter, enough to deglaze pot.)* Add the chicken, potatoes, and enough water to cover the chicken. *(Use hand to measure amount of water like Uncle Roger mum. Add dry curry leaf now if using.)* Bring the broth to a low boil and cook the chicken for about 30 minutes. *(Uncle Roger mum sometime cover wok for soupier texture. Other time she like to leave wok uncovered to make just a little thicker—Uncle Roger favorite way.)*

Add the 2 stalks smashed lemongrass, cover the wok, and gently boil for about 15 minutes.

Add the coconut cream, sugar, and 2 teaspoons salt and gently boil the curry, uncovered this time, for another 15 minutes; don't boil too hard at this point or the coconut cream may split. Adjust the seasonings with sugar or salt.

Serve the curry with the rice, noodles, or roti canai.

✕ HAIYAA . . .

Fresh curry leaf taste very *fresh*, musky, and little bit citrusy. Go to Southeast Asian or Indian market and buy a lot to freeze; also check freezer section. Fine, use dried if nothing else.

✓ FUIYOH!

Uncle Roger love smashing lemongrass to release aromatic oil, so satisfying. Peel and bash stalk with side of cleaver or meat mallet or bang with heavy pot. It OK to be noisy when cooking.

MALAYSIAN MEAT CURRY POWDER

If you don't have this in your pantry, it will be your new favorite curry powder. Most curry powder more yellow (from turmeric), this one more red because have so much dried chilli. (FUIYOH!) Come in blends for fish, vegetable, and meat. (Meat also mean chicken.) Look for brand like Baba's or Alagappa's. Worth it to buy online if don't have at local Asian store. (Probably not, unless shop is Malaysian.)

SANTAN

Real coconut cream is called santan (usually just say "coconut cream" on label). Not the same as thick separated fat on top of can of old coconut milk, watery cream of coconut, or even some can labeled "coconut cream" at Western store. Santan texture is silky and taste like fresh coconut. Even some Asian brand like Savoy sell two type of coconut cream in almost identical can, one diluted with water, one pure coconut, to trick customer. (Read ingredient label.) Niece and nephew want 99% coconut cream if can find it. If not, just use any thick canned coconut cream. Even Asian people probably won't notice.

田中式

NOODLES

UNCLE ROGER LOVE NOODLE. THEY BIG, BEAUTIFUL BOWLS OF COMFORT. RAMEN (PAGE 138), PAD THAI (PAGE 154), PHO (PAGE 156), PAN MEE. (ACTUALLY, RUN OUT OF ROOM TO PUT FAVORITE PAN MEE RECIPE IN THIS CHAPTER, UNCLE ROGER SAVE FOR NEXT BOOK.) ALWAYS REMEMBER MOST IMPORTANT RULE OF ANY NOODLE DISH: DON'T OVERCOOK YOUR NOODLE! NOBODY WANT SOGGY, GUMMY NOODLE THAT GO LIMP. (SORRY CHILDREN.)

RAMEN

Proper ramen have five component: broth, tare, noodle, topping, aroma oil. Every single one have to be perfect otherwise the balance of flavor will be off. We all know how precise Japanese people like their food, and there a whole cult following of ramen maker on the internet. You think Uncle Roger strict about fry rice? Wait till you meet these ramen experts. Uncle Roger is not a Ramen Master, but very proud of my Iekei Ramen (page 140) and components on the next pages. Give them a try, let Uncle Roger know what you think.

CAPTIVEAIRE
Morning

UNCLE ROGER'S IEKEI RAMEN

(pronounced E-A-K)

MAKES 2 RAMEN BOWLS *(Western cookbook always say to make too much ramen at one time. Keep your broth, tare, and chashu in refrigerator, have enough for at least 6 bowls. Eat all week.)*

Nephew James Chant is a ramen artist based in Cardiff, Wales. The unlikeliest place for ramen, but it amazing because he devote his whole life to the art of ramen. Uncle Roger respect that. Now Nephew James have successful ramen shop called Matsudai Ramen. In my 4 million subscriber special weejio, we make ramen together. Uncle Roger learn a lot of good ramen lessons from Nephew James, then I go home and perfect my own version here. This probably the only recipe in whole book YOU DON'T COOK WITH FEELING. I repeat. This one, DO NOT COOK WITH FEELING. Japanese ancestor will hate you.

4 cups Tonkotsu Ramen Broth (page 144)

6 to 8 thin slices Uncle Roger's Chashu (page 146)

6 ounces fresh or frozen ramen noodles *(no soba noodle like Jamie Oliver!)*

ASSEMBLY *(Remember, this serve 2 people. We will cut ingredient in half when assemble each bowl.)*

2 tablespoon plus 2 teaspoons Tare (page 150)

About 1½ tablespoons Aromatic Oil (recipe follows)

About 12 ounces Asian spinach *(Japanese or Taiwanese both good)*, **blanched or steamed and squeezed dry**

2 Ajitsuke Eggs (page 153), halved lengthwise

2 scallions, sliced *(Haiyaa, no white part for ramen, just green part for garnish.)*

2 sheets nori

Rewarm the tonkotsu ramen broth over low heat and prepare to boil the noodles. *(This mean have pot of water at a boil. Follow instruction on package. Japanese are such perfectionist, only people Uncle Roger trust on noodle cooking time.)*

Rewarm the chashu. *(Just read my instruction at end of chashu recipe, Uncle Roger already wrote this down, haiyaa.)*

When ready to serve . . . *(Are all of ramen component ready? Have two proper wide, deep ramen bowl? OK, NOW boil your noodle. Watch time closely! Drain.)*

Recipe continues

TO ASSEMBLE

(Remember, proper order is tare first, THEN oil, broth, noodle, toppings.) To each of two bowls, add 1 tablespoon plus 1 teaspoon of tare followed by 2½ teaspoons of aromatic oil. Add 2 cups of tonkotsu ramen broth, then divide the noodles between the bowls. Tuck half the spinach off to one side of each bowl and on the opposite side, slightly overlap Uncle Roger's chashu. *(Fan out pork slices so they look pretty.)* Divide the scallion greens and eggs between the bowls and right before serving, lay a sheet of nori over the edge. *(Tilt sheet off corner of bowl or seaweed will get soggy from broth, haiyaa.)*

Serve the ramen immediately. *(Slurp noodle with broth, mmm. Pick up chashu with chopstick!)*

× *HAIYAA . . .*

Ramen noodle must be alkaline noodle! That mean it have sodium bicarbonate (baking soda) in ingredient or it is NOT ramen noodle.

Want 3 to 4 slices chashu per bowl. Less, and it mean you run cheap ramen shop. Sorry, Uncle Roger know the photo here show two slices. That because Uncle Roger hungry and ate the third slice before photo taken.

No spork to eat ramen like Nigella Lawson! She famous chef, can afford to buy soup spoon and use it with her chopstick to eat ramen.

✓ *FUIYOH!*

Yes, it take a few days to make all Iekei ramen component—broth, chashu, tare, oil, and marinated egg. Go ahead and blanch spinach and make your aroma oil, keep everything in refrigerator. Now the easy part: Boil noodle, assemble ramen whenever hungry.

AROMATIC OIL

For oil, Uncle Roger use pork fat from making my chashu because go so well with tonkotsu pork bone broth. And it free. (FUIYOH!) Some ramen shop use chicken fat for Iekei ramen. Pick what you like.

Makes about 5 tablespoons, enough for 6 ramen bowls

5 tablespoons pork fat reserved from making Uncle Roger's Chashu (page 146), Pork Lard (store-bought or homemade, page 42), or rendered chicken fat

1 scallion, thinly sliced *(Whole scallion this time, we are going to fry onion.)*

2 garlic cloves, thinly sliced

In a small saucepan, heat the pork fat over medium heat until hot but not smoking. Add the scallions and garlic and fry until golden brown. *(Nice dark brown color give oil flavor.)* Take the saucepan off the heat and when the fat is cool, strain.

Cover and refrigerate the aromatic oil for up to 2 weeks. Rewarm over low heat.

Weejios

Uncle Roger Recreate Jamie Oliver Ramen

Uncle Roger Make Ramen (with James Chant of @matsudairamen; 4M Subscriber Special)

TONKOTSU RAMEN BROTH

MAKES ABOUT 12 CUPS (3 QUARTS), ENOUGH FOR 5 TO 6 RAMEN BOWLS

(Exact quantity of broth you get depend on water evaporation.)

Throw some animal bone and a few other ingredient into a pot, boil, have ramen broth. Sound easy, but nothing Japanese people do is easy. Difference between sad, thin Western bone broth and Japanese tonkotsu broth for Iekei ramen on page right before this is how they are made. Western chef very gently simmer bone and aromatics for only a few hours, why it look and taste like dirty water with a hint of animal bone. Good tonkotsu broth very light, almost milky color, richer consistency, and better flavor than ANY Western bone broth because Ramen Master boil the hell out of bones (mainly pork) for hours and hours. In Japan, some chef boil tonkotsu broth for days. That process dissolve every bit of collagen, tissue, marrow, fat, and flavor from bone so it all end up in broth.

Uncle Roger too busy making weejio to sit by stove so long while ramen broth cook. A good compromise I learned from Nephew James is to soak the bones overnight. (Nephew James do this when he make ramen with Uncle Roger. Make very good broth. Uncle Roger tweak recipe, use chicken paw for more gelatin, add a few more authentic aromatic ingredient.) After long soak, boil the bones first very quickly then rinse off all brown muck that makes the broth cloudy. Start over with clean water and now boil the broth for about four hours to get nice, rich, clean ramen broth. Uncle Roger let my broth chill overnight with bone for even more flavor, strain the next day. Now ready to make ramen anytime. FUIYOH!

2 pounds assorted pork bones *(best to have a mix of back and neck bones)*

1½ pounds pork leg bones

1 pound chicken paws *(Western people say feet. If can't get paw, bone OK, read Uncle Roger note.)*

3- to 4-ounce piece pork back fat *(This what it sound like, from back of pig, almost all fat. Get at Asian or Latino market.)*

4 dried whole shiitake mushrooms

½ medium yellow or white onion

1 large or 2 small Japanese negi onions or Western leeks, cleaned of grit

3- to 4-inch knob ginger, unpeeled and sliced into thick pieces *(length of your finger)*

1 head garlic

In a large bowl, combine the pork bones (assorted and leg) and enough cold water to generously cover. In a separate bowl or container, cover the chicken feet with water to cover. Refrigerate all of the bones overnight. *(Don't roast bones like Jamie Oliver! Will give ramen broth dirty brown color, supposed to be light.)*

The next day, drain the pork and chicken feet. *(Just partly cover your drain and dump out into the sink.)* Put both in a large stockpot, add enough water to cover, bring to vigorous boil over high heat, and immediately drain. Clean the stockpot.

Pick out the chicken feet, rinse well, and return them to the stockpot. *(If using chicken bones, need to really clean them like the pork bone. Read next paragraph.)*

Rinse the pork bones well. *(Rinse off ALL the brown muck. Don't want that in ramen broth.)* Stick your finger into the bone cavities to dislodge the dark bone marrow inside. *(Chopstick also help.)* Rinse the pork bones again and return them to the stockpot.

Add 5 quarts (20 cups) water to the stockpot *(or however much water fit in pot, can add more later when stock reduce . . .)* and bring to a boil. Skim off any foam that rises to the surface for the first 5 minutes. *(If niece and nephew did good job cleaning bones, should be a lot less foam than usual.)* Add the pork back fat, shiitake mushrooms, yellow or white onion, negi onions or leeks, ginger, and garlic *(no salt!)* and bring the water back to a boil. *(This not the time to be gentle. Must have a good, solid boil for best ramen broth.)* Boil the broth, uncovered, for about 4 hours; as it reduces, add another 8 cups water. *(If no room in your little pot for all the water at the beginning, remember to add it now, too, as broth cooks down. Need a LOT of water to properly reduce and thicken broth.)* Let cool and refrigerate the broth and bones, without straining, overnight. *(Why are Western people so concerned about covering bowl in refrigerator all the time? Pork bone broth infuse everything with delicious pork flavor.)*

The next day, return the congealed broth and bones to the pot and bring to a low boil. *(When broth is chilled, can see all the good gelatin.)* Strain the broth, in batches if needed, through a fine-mesh sieve. *(So much work to use fine-mesh sieve if you have one but worth it. Push down on ingredient a little bit as you strain, this extract every last bit of flavor.)* You should have about 12 cups (3 quarts) of broth; if the broth reduced substantially more, add a little water only if you need more servings of ramen. *(Less broth mean you have even better flavor!)*

When cool, refrigerate the broth for up to 1 week. *(Freeze broth in individual portion, now have broth to make ramen anytime.)*

✔ FUIYOH!

Chicken paw have every quality Uncle Roger like: good collagen, clean, and cheap. And it have very little blood, so it keep broth light in color. If no feet at your store, a mix of chicken neck bones and wings are OK. Neck bones have less gelatin and must clean well because bones have more sinew and blood.

Weejios

Uncle Roger Recreate Jamie Oliver Ramen

Uncle Roger Make Ramen (with James Chant of @matsudairamen; 4M Subscriber Special)

UNCLE ROGER'S CHASHU

MAKES ENOUGH FOR ABOUT 8 RAMEN BOWLS, WITH LEFTOVERS

(Leftover chashu good in fry rice!)

When Uncle Roger live in the UK, I make Jamie Oliver terrible version of ramen with Nephew James Chant at his restaurant Matsudai Ramen. Jamie Olive Oil chashu so white! No flavor or color, all sad and falling apart. (EMOTIONAL DAMAGE . . .)

A good chashu is brown, beautiful, and sexy. Remember: Japanese Ramen Master is always perfecting his craft. Nobody else going to ever make chashu as good. That OK. Try mine. All the aunties tell Uncle Roger my chashu roll is nice and thick, have the perfect tenderness and flavor. (Children reading, don't say that to your school friend.)

3- to 3¼-pound slab skinless pork belly, like Japanese Kurobuta *(Want a nice meaty piece, not Chinese-style belly for this. It have too much fat.)*

MARINADE

- **1 large Japanese negi onion or Western leek**
- **1 cup soy sauce**
- **1 cup sake**
- **1 cup mirin**
- **½ cup granulated sugar**
- **4 to 5 thick coins of ginger, unpeeled** *(Peel add flavor.)*
- **2 to 3 garlic cloves, unpeeled**

(Start chashu at least 2 day before you want to eat it, in case need to marinate chashu longer.) Preheat the oven to 350°F (180°C).

Trim the pork belly into a rectangle roughly 8 to 9 inches long. *(Exact size doesn't matter. It's your method that count. Make nice shape for tight roll.)* Save the pork scraps for another use. *(Uncle Roger freeze any uncooked pork belly scraps until I have enough to make my Cantonese-style Sweet and Sour Pork, page 195.)*

Lay the pork belly on the counter vertically with the meatiest end closest to you. Cut a piece of butcher's twine a few finger joints (inches) longer than the slab. Put the twine underneath the slab, roll up the pork belly into a tight roll, and tie the string. Secure the roll with 4 to 5 more pieces of twine. *(Western people make this too complicated, call it trussing. Nobody going to see your knots. Just tie each knot, cut off ends of twine. Simple.)* Trim any overhanging pieces of pork from the sides of the roll.

Recipe continues

In a large cast-iron or other skillet *(pork roll too big for a wok)*, sear the pork roll until light golden brown on all sides. *(Don't rush. Pretend you are Japanese shokunin, a master craftsman.)* Save the pork fat.

MARINADE

Trim the negi onion or the leek, reserving only the whole green stalk. *(Western people always think white part of leek the best. Green stalk have so much flavor.)* Cut the stalk in half lengthwise and rinse out the grit.

In a saucepot or wok, combine the soy sauce, sake, mirin, sugar, and 1½ cups water. Bring to a low boil, stir to dissolve the sugar, and turn off the heat.

Find an ovenproof deep medium saucepot that will fairly snugly fit the pork roll and marinade. *(Nothing too big and wide. Want marinade to cover at least three-quarters of pork roll. Even stainless steel mixing bowl work, don't need fancy pot.)* Add the pork roll and pork fat and tuck the negi onion stalk, ginger, and garlic around the pork. Cover the pot tightly with foil and poke 10 to 12 holes in the foil with a chopstick, then move the chopstick around in a circle to make each hole slightly bigger. *(We are making a homemade otoshibuta, Japanese drop lid, let out steam but keep marinade from evaporating too fast.)*

Reduce the oven temperature to 250°F (120°C) and bake the pork for 2 hours.

Flip the pork roll and bake until a small knife easily slides through without the meat falling apart, about 2 more hours. Let the pork cool in the marinade.

Transfer the pork and marinade to a smaller loaf pan or bowl so the pork roll is mostly submerged, cover, and refrigerate for 12 to 18 hours. *(Taste after 12 hour, see if you like chashu. If not, marinate a few hour longer. You are Ramen Master now.)*

Scoop off the pork fat on top of the marinade and refrigerate the fat for up to 1 week. *(Do NOT throw out pork fat, haiyaa. Put it in refrigerator until ready to make your Aromatic Oil on page 143. If forget, that OK, can use my homemade Pork Lard on page 42 or buy some.)* Strain the chashu marinade and refrigerate for up to 1 week to make Tare (page 150) and the Ajitsuke Eggs (page 153).

Wrap the chashu in plastic and refrigerate for at least 8 hours or up to 5 days before slicing or freeze. *(Freeze in smaller chunks, easy to thaw, cut a few slices for bowl of ramen.)*

To slice and rewarm the chashu for ramen: *(Is your knife sharp? Sharpen it now. Is chashu WELL chilled? Pop in freezer for 30 minute. If slice chashu while hot like Jamie Oliver, it gonna break apart, you end up with pulled pork, haiyaa.)* Trim off one end of the chashu. Very thinly slice the chashu roughly ⅛ inch thick. *(Smooth motion with knife so get nice thin, uniform pieces. If pieces too thick, Uncle Roger won't go back to your ramen-ya. Mean you lack skill.)* Only slice as much chashu as you need.

To rewarm the chashu, heat a small amount of Tonkotsu Ramen Broth (page 144) or other low-sodium broth in a skillet just until warm. *(This only time Uncle Roger use low-sodium chicken broth, and ONLY if I don't have enough ramen broth. Don't want to mess up delicate flavor of chashu with too much sodium.)* Add the chashu and gently warm the pork over low heat. *(Not too long! Take chashu out of broth as soon as warm so you don't affect texture. Uncle Roger like to now blast my chashu with blow torch. Get a little light char on pork fat at edges of each slice.)*

× HAIYAA . . .

NEVER throw away chashu marinade! You work so hard to get that rich flavor with pork fat bonus for extra cholesterol and mouthfeel. Keep for Tare (page 150) and Ajitsuke Eggs (page 153). And save pork fat for your Aromatic Oil (page 143) or to fry up rice or any protein.

✓ FUIYOH!

Japanese Korubuta (breed is called Berkshire in West) have delicious flavor, tender meat, nice marbling. Perfect for chashu roll. Get meatier piece or niece and nephew will be gnawing on pure fat.

When Uncle Roger want chashu but too lazy to make ramen broth, I make chashu don. Steam some rice, top with sliced chashu, Uncle Roger's Crispy Fried Egg (page 54), pickled ginger, sesame seed, and nori.

Chop up any (cooked!) scraps and end pieces from your chashu roll. Fry up pork pieces instead of lap cheong* in Uncle Roger's Egg Fry Rice (page 38) or my Cheap and Easy XO Fry Rice (page 43).

Weejios

Uncle Roger Recreate Jamie Oliver Ramen

Uncle Roger Make Ramen (with James Chant of @matsudairamen; 4M Subscriber Special)

*Homemade chashu the ONLY acceptable substitute for Chinese sausage in Uncle Roger fry rice.

TARE

(with chashu marinade, so delicious)

MAKES ABOUT ¾ CUP (12 TABLESPOONS), ENOUGH FOR 6 TO 8 RAMEN BOWLS

Tare from best ramen shop is like bonsai tree. Aged for a very long time. Ramen Master scoop out some of old tare, use it when cook new batch. For Iekei-style ramen, good noodle chef save marinade from chashu to use in marinade, just like Uncle Roger. Give tare a bigger flavor than most home cook tare.

- **Fine table salt**
- **MSG, King of Flavor**
- **½ cup marinade reserved from Uncle Roger's Chashu (page 146)**
- **½ cup soy sauce**
- **1 piece kombu** *(length of your finger and width of hand)*
- **1 dried shiitake mushroom**

In a small saucepan, combine the marinade, soy sauce, kombu, shiitake mushroom, ¼ cup water, and 2 to 3 pinches each of salt and MSG and bring to a low boil. Gently boil the tare until reduced by about one-quarter, about 10 minutes. When cool, refrigerate the tare overnight or for a more intense flavor, 1 to 2 days. Remove the kombu and strain the tare. *(Squeeze all the liquid out of shiitake back into tare, give umami boost.)*

Refrigerate the tare for up to 2 weeks. *(This tare is not good to keep for whole year because it have those delicious pork juices in it. Might get food poisoning and die.)*

× HAIYAA . . .

Ramen without Tare is like Uncle Roger without orange polo. Tare give broth all the salty and umami flavors. Tare give the broth soul.

BOILED EGGS

(hard or soft, however you like it . . .)

MAKES AS MANY BOILED EGGS AS YOU WANT

So many type of boil egg. Uncle Roger love a jammy soft-boil egg for my ramen and a little runnier soft-boil egg for my Nasi Lemak (page 184). Auntie Shakila like firm-boil egg for her Fuchka (page 77). We all different. Especially with softer boiled egg, you need patience of a Ramen Master to get it perfectly peeled. (Softer the yolk, the more delicate the whites.) That OK for things like ramen. You are slicing the egg in half, so easy to cover up little nicks in whites, try harder next time.

Large eggs *(Just grab some egg out of refrigerator, don't need Uncle Roger to tell you exactly how many for recipe, haiyaa. If only have small egg, remember it will cook up faster.)*

✔ FUIYOH!

Older eggs always best for boiling, have air pocket. A little bit easier to peel than young eggs.

Fill a bowl with ice water. *(We gonna make cold plunge but for egg.)*

In a pot large enough to fit the eggs in a single layer, bring enough water to a boil that will fully cover the eggs. *(Need enough water to cover egg but not too much, or weight of egg will make hot water overflow from pot.)* **With a spider or spoon, carefully but quickly add the eggs to the pot a few at a time.** *(Slide each egg GENTLY into pot or egg will crack. With big wok ladle can add 2 egg at a time.)*

Immediately set the timer for 6 minutes *(soft-boiled egg with more runny yolk)*, **7 to 8 minutes** *(soft-boiled with a jammy yolk)*, **10 minutes** *(hard-boiled with a deep yellow, creamy yolk)*, **or 11 to 12 minutes** *(light yellow yolk with a crumbly texture)*. **Once the water returns to a boil, reduce the heat if it boils too vigorously or the shells may crack. Transfer the eggs to the ice bath.** *(Some auntie say must peel egg under running water after just a minute in ice bath to make it easier. Other auntie peel egg later, when need it, say it keep egg fresh longer. Uncle Roger not sure who is right. Egg so hard to peel perfectly anyway, haiyaa.)*

Refrigerate the boiled eggs for up to 1 week; cover the eggs if they have been peeled.

AJITSUKE EGGS

(also with chashu marinade)

MAKES 8 CURED EGGS, ENOUGH FOR 8 RAMEN BOWLS

(Always boil a few extra egg as insurance. Some not as pretty when peel, or crack when add to pot. Eat those for snack, FUIYOH!)

When Uncle Roger watch weejio of Jamie Oliver making his ajitsuke egg marinade, Jamie add a "splash" of mirin like he making cocktail, haiyaa. Good ajitsuke egg marinade need a LOT of mirin, sake, and soy sauce to balance flavors. Most home cook recipes so wasteful, throw out leftover marinade from making chashu, haiyaa. Chashu marinade already have all the extra sugar (mirin also sweet) you need and come with a nice, fatty pork belly flavor. Perfect for my ramen egg.

About 1 cup marinade reserved from Uncle Roger's Chashu (page 146)

½ cup soy sauce

¼ cup sake *(Don't waste money on expensive brand, get covered up by soy sauce.)*

¼ cup mirin

8 Boiled Eggs (page 151; *soft boiled with very jammy yolk, 7 minute is perfect)*

In a measuring cup or bowl, combine the marinade, soy sauce, sake, and mirin. Put the peeled eggs in jars or a container that will fit them fairly snugly and pour the marinade on top; the eggs should be completely submerged. *(If not enough marinade, add a little chashu marinade to cover egg.)*

Fold a paper towel into a square and lay it on top of the eggs. *(This is old home-cook trick so your egg not gonna have white unmarinated spot on top.)* Cover and refrigerate the eggs for 6 to 12 hours, then discard the curing liquid. *(Length of time is up to you. The longer niece and nephew leave egg in marinade, bigger the flavor but yolk cure longer. That mean yolk start to firm up more, like hard-boiled egg. If leave too long, yolk get rubbery. Sign of bad ramen shop.)*

Refrigerate the ajitsuke eggs for up to 5 days.

✔ FUIYOH!

If you read my ramen recipe all the way to here, congratulations! Uncle Roger impressed. Ramen is one of the most complex dishes to make. So many steps. It not just random noodles in some flavored broth. So next time you go eat at ramen restaurant, you can appreciate all the time and effort that go into this dish.

PAD THAI

It so hard to find a good pad Thai outside of Thailand, haiyaa. Uncle Roger review so many bad version in my weejios, from Rachael Ray dumping shit everywhere to Jamie Oliver diarrhea sauce and even a Dollar Store pad Thai that still make me cry. The reason pad Thai is so terrible in the West is people leave out too many authentic ingredient, then try to cover up mistake with too much sugar, not enough sour flavor, noodle too wet and soggy with sauce, or no char from wok hei. Not to mention they use wrong tofu, wrong tamarind paste, wrong radish, haiyaa.

Since then I learn how hard it is to get one very important ingredient outside of Asia: Thai sweet preserved radish called chai po waan. (This is the sweet pickled radish, not the salty Thai preserved radish. Radish is very confusing ingredient to white people.) You must live in a city with a very good Thai or Southeast Asian market, or buy it online. (Online usually expensive for little radish.) Even one of Uncle Roger favorite Thai aunties, Pailin Chongchitnant, say Thai preserved radish is "optional" and offer pickled Japanese radish (takuan) as substitute in her cookie weejio.

Uncle Roger have open mind, so I go buy this Japanese radish that Auntie Pailin talk about and do a taste test with the Thai radish. (OK, OK, name is similar, maybe it will be good.) Thai pickled radish is a little bit sweet and salty, really elevate pad Thai with a depth of flavor, and have nice brown color that blend in with other ingredient. Japanese pickled radish is like Thai radish on acid trip. Taste like pure sugar and look fluorescent yellow like highlighter pen, haiyaa. (This auntie *very* good cook, so Uncle Roger forgive her. Go watch her weejio channel @PailinsKitchen if you want to learn to cook authentic Thai food.)

That why Uncle Roger refuse to put a pad Thai recipe in my book. It very, very hard to get it right if you live outside Thailand. So what can niece and nephew do? Go to Thailand, have auntie teach you how to make it. Remember all their secrets. Go home, open Asian market that ship cheap chai po waan all over Western world. You now the hero of pad Thai.

Weejios

Jamie Oliver's Worst Recipe Yet (Veggie Pad Thai)

Uncle Roger Found the Worst Pad Thai (Rachael Ray)

Uncle Roger Shocked by Dollar Store Pad Thai (William Osman)

Uncle Roger Love this Pad Thai (@Pailins Kitchen)

NIECE TWAY'S PHO

(from her stepdad, Kevin, FUIYOH!)

MAKES 8 LARGE BOWLS *(This serve more like ten Western people. Vietnamese people like a LOT of broth with their pho, keep coming back to the stove for more.)*

This is Vietnam national dish. Western people love to tell Asian people how much they love pho, but they pronounce it like "faux." Every Asian person want to laugh and say, "It pronounced FUH. Like Fuh-k off." But Asian people too nice to say that, so instead we smile and go watch Uncle Roger weejios on WORST pho ever. (Jamie Oliver and Rachael Ray win. Again.)

Pho can be as intricate, nuanced, and complex as the best bowls of ramen. The broth have so many different flavor, all working together in harmony: savory, sweet, peppery, fragrant. The noodles are light and soak up the broth, and the meat tender. Uncle Roger have some of the best pho I ever eat when I kidnap Nephew Loan Shark by putting out sign for free Vietnamese coffee. (Vietnamese coffee trap the oldest trick in book.) Usually Vietnamese restaurant look like shit, smell like shit, but the food taste amazing. Didi WeHo in Los Angeles very pretty and smell so clean, even name sound fancy. Uncle Roger expecting watered down Asian food. But Niece Tway (Tue Nguyen, the owner of Didi West Hollywood, she go by @TwayDabae) is the real deal. Her pho is FUIYOH!

Kevin is my stepdad, who happens to be an amazing cook. And I'm proud of his pho. His recipe is special to my entire family and it's the only entry in my cookbook, Di An, *that isn't completely mine. I did not make any changes to it because I genuinely think it's perfect as it is. In 2019, this bowl of pho single-handedly saved my family's Vietnamese restaurant in Thousand Oaks, California, from closing. All bias aside: This is, hands down, the best pho I've ever tasted.* —Tue

Kosher or fine table salt *(Niece Tway use kosher salt. Uncle Roger too cheap for that so I give you my table salt equivalent.)*

BEEF AND BROTH *(Uncle Roger make broth and meat on weekend, eat pho all week.)*

10 pounds beef bones *(Get at Asian market, Western butcher too expensive. Mix of marrow and neck bones good, but get whatever they have.)*

About 1½ pounds whole flank steak, trimmed *(This not fajita, haiyaa. Want whole piece, thick as you can get for nice slices. Uncle Roger like a lot of meat, I cook more than Niece Tway. It shrink when you cook it.)*

About 1½ pounds beef brisket, trimmed *(Flat-cut brisket best for slicing, point-cut also work, cut into chunks. You choose. If have thick fat cap, get bigger piece so have enough meat when trim off fat.)*

AROMATICS

5- to 6-inch piece ginger, unpeeled *(Big! Roughly length of hand.)*

1 large yellow or white onion, unpeeled

5 to 6 small Asian or 2 medium Western shallots, unpeeled

5 green cardamom pods

3 cinnamon sticks

5 whole star anise

2 tablespoons whole cloves

1 tablespoon coriander seeds

2½ teaspoons fennel seeds

PHO BROTH

About ¾ cup rock sugar, or ½ cup granulated sugar

About 7 tablespoons mushroom bouillon powder *(Lee Kum Kee good.)*

4½ tablespoons beef-flavored pho soup base *(Get Cốt Phở Bò brand or Niece Tway will pound Uncle Roger with her mallet.)*

3 bunches scallions *(Chop off white parts with your cleaver for broth, save green parts for garnish.)*

TO SERVE

Reserved scallion stalks, sliced *(Niece Tway use every bit of scallion, nothing wasted.)*

3 bunches cilantro, leaves and tender top stems only, chopped

3 to 4 Western limes, sliced

8 to 10 ounces (about 2 cups) mung bean sprouts, more if you like

4 to 5 jalapeños, thinly sliced

Pickled Garlic Vinegar (recipe follows)

3 (14- to 16-ounce) packages pho noodles *(Medium thick, like linguini, not vermicelli rice stick. Pho noodle usually come in pack of three, make enough noodle for 2 or 3 bowl per package. Boil more noodle to feed bigger family.)*

Recipe continues

BEEF AND BROTH *(Broth and beef take long time to cook. Make on weekend, have pho all week.)*

In a *(very!)* large stockpot, combine the beef bones, 10 quarts water, and 1 tablespoon kosher salt or 1½ teaspoons fine salt. *(Niece Tway have very BIG pot like every Asian auntie that can fit 2½ gallon of water and heavy bone. If have little Western stockpot, fill up with as much water as you can, add more later.)* Bring the water to a vigorous boil *(turn up heat to high!)* and immediately drain and rinse the bones with cold water. *(Clean out pot, going to use again. One less dish to wash.)*

Return the beef bones to the pot and add another 10 quarts water. *(Or as much water as you can, this time you can add the rest after water level cook down.)* Add 5 tablespoons kosher salt or 2½ tablespoons fine salt; remember the water level for later.

(Did you forget to trim off any large pieces of fat and silver skin from flank steak and brisket?) Add both meats to the pot, bring to a vigorous boil, and reduce the heat to medium-low. *(Lower heat if you have powerful stove burner, FUIYOH!)* Cover the pot and cook for about 4 hours; occasionally skim off any impurities that float to the surface of the broth. *(If you have small pot, remember to add the rest of your water as the broth cook down. Use time while broth cook to take nap, char your aromatic and toast spices in next step.)*

AROMATICS

While the meat cooks, toast the ginger, onion, and shallots directly over the open flame of a gas stove, grill, or open fire *(like ancestor, FUIYOH!)*; the skin should be blackened on all sides and the first layer of flesh slightly softened. *(Chopstick burn, use tongs or metal skewer.)* To use a broiler, cut the onion in half so it lays flat on a sheet pan. *(Toasting the ginger, onion, and shallot to get dark color very important for broth flavor. Don't cut corner. Broiler is last resort, take very long time.)*

Transfer the aromatics to a bowl and cover with cold water for a few minutes to remove some *(not all!)* of the char, then drain. *(Washing charred aromatics going to get Uncle Roger in trouble with some Vietnamese aunties. Some like to wash off a little of char, some like to leave it all on for more toasty broth flavor. You are the chef.)* Smash the ginger *(kill it with mallet like Uncle Roger, pot also good . . .)*. Peel the onion and shallots and set aside with the ginger.

In a large mortar, pound the cardamom to break open the pods and discard the skins. Add the cinnamon sticks and pound a few times to release the oils. *(Just smash, get out aggression. Bigger pieces OK, we are not grinding.)*

Heat a dry skillet over high heat until very hot; it should smoke. Reduce the heat to low and toast the cardamom and cinnamon until very fragrant. *(Stir! Don't want to burn but toast at least 1 minute, maybe 2 minute.)* Add the star anise, cloves, coriander seeds, and fennel seeds, and stir until fragrant, about 30 seconds. Transfer the spices to a tea ball or tie them up in cheesecloth. *(Cheesecloth so fancy. This how you know Niece Tway real chef.)*

PHO BROTH

When the meat is ready, use tongs to remove the beef bones and discard. *(See how nice this broth is niece and nephew? Not too dark, and good flavor with layer of oil on top. Not like Jamie Oliver broth, haiyaa.)*

Add enough water to the pot to bring it roughly two inches beneath the original (10-quart) level; with the weight of the meat still in the pot, you should be adding about 8 quarts of water. *(This why you remember the water level in pot. Very good technique, all about feeling. Measure water if not sure. Don't want to mess up broth now.)* Add the rock sugar, mushroom bouillon powder, and beef-flavored pho soup base, stir, and return to a boil. After a few minutes, skim off any impurities that float to the surface of the broth.

Recipe continues

Drop the charred ginger, onion, and shallot into pot and add the scallion whites and toasted spices *(in your tea ball or fancy cheesecloth).* Boil the broth, uncovered, for at least 30 minutes or for up to 1 hour. *(Not too vigorous now. Gentle boil to infuse broth with flavor of aromatic.)* Scoop out the scallion whites, charred yellow onion, shallots, and ginger, and spice pouch. Adjust the seasonings with mushroom bouillon powder *(this add saltiness)* or sugar. *(If have rock sugar, be patient, it take a while to melt.)*

Cover the pot and keep the broth warm over low heat until ready to serve or let the broth and beef cool and refrigerate overnight. *(Take beef out of broth when cool, refrigerate in separate container. Now Uncle Roger ready to slice off only as much beef I need.)*

(Finally, ready to eat.)

TO SERVE

Rewarm the broth and meat over low heat, if needed. In another pot, heat enough water to cook the noodles.

Remove the flank steak and brisket from the broth and slice both against the grain into strips. *(Uncle Roger like to slice my flank steak and cut my brisket into meaty chunks, how I have it when I go to Niece Tway's restaurant in weejio. Good texture contrast. Put brisket pieces in broth, fan out flank steak slices on top. I always slice flank steak at a diagonal to get wider strip to pick up with chopstick.)*

Arrange the reserved chopped scallion stalks, cilantro, limes, mung bean sprouts, jalapeños, and pickled garlic vinegar on a serving platter so guests can add as much as they want to their soup. *(Niece Tway use such fancy language in cookbook. No such thing as guest at Vietnamese restaurant. They are all hungry customer ready to judge your food.)*

Cook the noodles according to the package directions and drain. *(This recipe from Niece Tway, she seem to believe in Asian packaging instructions. Uncle Roger more skeptical. Remember to use your judgment, don't blindly follow instruction.)*

Divide the noodles among eight large serving bowls. Arrange several flank steak and brisket slices *(or chunks of brisket)* off to one side of each bowl. Ladle enough hot broth over the meat and noodles to cover both. *(Use feeling! People will get more broth if they want it.)* Serve the pho with the toppings.

× HAIYAA . . .

No complaining to Uncle Roger about how long good pho take to make. It like Auntie Shakila's Biryani (page 208), worth the wait. Clean your house while you make broth. Put a podcast on. Find some weejios for Uncle Roger to review, send me a message.

Jamie Oliver screw up everything about pho, even the cut of meat. (Skirt steak too thin and tough, can only cut scrawny little pieces.) Flank steak is thicker, so when you slice at a diagonal, get pieces to pick up with chopstick. Flat-cut brisket come in smaller cuts, perfect for this, but bigger chunk of whole brisket that you cut up yourself OK. Freeze extra to make pho again.

Weejios

Uncle Roger Recreate Jamie Oliver Pho . . . Big Mistake! (with @TwayDabae and Nephew Loan Shark @WillPepperComedy)

Uncle Roger FORCED to Review Jamie Oliver's Pho

Uncle Roger Make Pho

Uncle Roger Hate British TV Pho

PICKLED GARLIC VINEGAR

Garlic vinegar for pho called dam toi. Tiny little spoonful of sweet vinegar brighten pho flavor. Niece Tway like to add a few slices of the pickled garlic to her pho. FUIYOH!

Makes 1 cup, plenty for the pho *(Keep leftover in refrigerator for next time make pho.)*

½ cup distilled white vinegar

⅓ cup granulated sugar

1 head garlic, peeled and thinly sliced

In a small saucepan, combine the vinegar, sugar, and ¼ cup water, bring to a gentle boil, and stir to dissolve the sugar. Remove the saucepan from the heat.

Put the garlic in a 1 cup or larger container. When the pickling liquid is completely cool, pour it over the garlic.

Refrigerate the pickled garlic vinegar overnight or for up to 2 weeks; the garlic flavors will intensify as the vinegar ages. *(Some aunties keep their pickled garlic in refrigerator for months. Niece Tway like young garlic, not too aged.)*

LA CORNUE

CURRIES

SO MANY ASIAN CULTURES HAVE THEIR OWN VERSION OF CURRY. UNCLE ROGER LOVE THEM ALL, BUT IN THIS BOOK WE ONLY HAVE SPACE TO COVER THAI- AND MALAYSIAN-STYLE CURRY. THESE CURRY ALL PACK WITH FULL-BODIED FLAVOR. YOU GONNA LOVE IT.

THAI CURRY PASTE

(ARE YOU READY FOR SOME POUNDING?)

In Thailand, if you want to make curry, you go buy good, fresh paste. (Or just go buy curry—Uncle Roger mean the dish—from hawker, no reason to even make it. Theirs always better than yours.) Hawker at wet market have giant bowls filled with all different type of curry paste: green, red, yellow, sour, massaman, panang. At Western grocery store, curry paste taste either rancid or bland. Bad flavor, color, smell. If you want good, jarred curry paste, must buy from Asian market. But if you want something even better, make Uncle Roger green (see page 166) and red (see page 168) curry pastes fresh. Bonus point is that you will impress all the aunties with your pounding skills.

Before niece and nephew start, very important to remember: We are making a PASTE. Need a big mortar to hold all the ingredients and must keep pounding until smooth. A blender require water (paste will get too wet, haiyaa) and a food processor only work if you are making a very big batch. Spice or coffee grinder that can handle wet ingredients works if you are lazy, but you have to chop everything up in small batches. Uncle Roger doesn't have expensive kitchen appliance. Might as well just keep pounding.

And, this last bit is for Jamie Olive Oil. Curry paste must have fresh galangal. If you use ginger, it is NOT Thai curry paste. Wrong book.

THAI GREEN CURRY WITH CHICKEN AND EGGPLANT

(Gaeng Kheow Wan Gai)

SERVES 4 OR 5

Thai green curry is one of Uncle Roger favorite dish in world. (Except when Jamie Oliver make it. That is sadness.) It such a rich, savory, spicy broth, and go so well with rice. In Thailand, so many different version. (Uncle Mark Wiens take me to eat one with little chunks of coagulated blood that tastes like tofu on crack, watch weejio.) This is the green curry Uncle Roger make when I am not in Thailand but want good Thai food. In the West, I can't always get the exact ingredient I need to make the most authentic curry. And even then, sometime even little herb like Thai basil at Asian market not as fragrant as those picked same day, like auntie get all over Thailand. My home version still very close to the real deal and so delicious.

Uncle Roger have two rules. You MUST make your own Thai green curry paste. And don't overdo the sugar and coconut milk! Too sweet, too coconut-y. Coconut milk is cheap way to stretch recipe, how Thai restaurant in West trick people to spend a lot of money on bad curry. Remember, this is Thai green curry, not Thai coconut soup. Don't make Jamie Oliver mistake.

Neutral oil, for frying

Fine table salt

MSG, King of Flavor

About 1¼ pounds boneless, skinless chicken thighs, cut into bite-size pieces

4 to 5 tablespoons coconut fat plus about ⅔ cup full-fat coconut milk, both from a 13.5-ounce can *(Boxed coconut OK, just don't shake can or box! Need fat separated.)*

About 1 cup Thai Green Curry Paste (page 166; *yes, need whole recipe for authentic flavor)*

About 2 cups chicken broth *(No low-sodium broth ever in real Asian cookbook! Rehydrated bouillon also good.)*

4 to 6 medium Thai eggplant, cut into bite-size pieces *(Not too many vegetable, haiyaa . . .)*

5 to 6 fresh makrut (kaffir) lime leaves, rolled and thinly sliced, or whole dried lime leaves *(Fresh sliced leaf best, dried leaf OK, must leave whole. Finely chopped Western lime peel, just green part, OK only in a pinch.)*

About 2½ tablespoons fish sauce

About 1 teaspoon coconut or palm sugar, or loosely packed light brown sugar

A big handful (1 cup loosely packed) of Thai basil leaves

TO SERVE

3 to 4 long (pinky-length) red Thai chillies, sliced *(green chilli only if that all you have)*

Steamed rice

Recipe continues

(Do you have all ingredient prepped and ready?) Season the chicken lightly with a few pinches of both salt and MSG.

Scoop out the fat on top of the can of coconut milk.

In a dry wok over medium heat, bring the coconut fat to a low boil. *(Dry wok should still be seasoned, have little slick of oil over surface always. If your wok is nonstick or bone-dry, a splash of oil before coconut fat.)* Cook the coconut cream until bubbling and slightly shiny from the oil separating, about 2 minutes; if the coconut cream starts to burn or the oil doesn't separate, add about 1 tablespoon oil. *(Process of separating oil from solids over high heat called "cracking" the coconut cream. Sometimes oil won't separate with can coconut, depend on brand. Fake it by adding a spoonful of vegetable oil.)*

Spread out the curry paste in the wok and stir occasionally until aromatic, about 2 minutes; if the paste starts to brown at the edges, add another splash of oil. *(Making curry like fry rice. Must trust yourself, use feeling.)* Add the chicken and toss and stir for a few seconds to coat the pieces in the paste, then add the chicken broth and ⅔ cup coconut milk and scrape any paste off the bottom of the wok. *(Resist the urge to add more coconut milk now. Western people have taken hold of your mind. Can adjust with more coconut milk later.)* Add the eggplant and lime leaves, bring to a low boil, and cook until the chicken and eggplant are tender, about 10 minutes.

Add the fish sauce, sugar, and 3 to 4 pinches of MSG, and stir until the sugar dissolves.

If needed, thin out the curry with a little broth or water. *(If curry isn't soupy enough, need to add liquid. Broth best, but a little water OK. Most important, don't dilute flavor! Remember, you will be eating this with rice, so it OK if the curry flavor just a little bit too strong. Steamed rice will dissipate flavor. Coconut milk only as last resort if truly need it!)* Adjust the seasonings with fish sauce, sugar, or salt.

Just before serving, stir the basil leaves into the curry. *(All go into curry. NO basil leaves on top!)*

TO SERVE

Spoon the curry into bowls, garnish with the red chillies, and serve with the steamed rice. *(Rice come on side so niece and nephew can mix in how much you want. Never go in same bowl as curry, haiyaa.)*

✕ HAIYAA . . .

Every eggplant is not the same! Thai green eggplant has earthy flavor, less sweet than Chinese, Japanese, or Italian. And, we are making GREEN curry. If you must substitute another eggplant, make it Asian variety.

✓ FUIYOH!

In Thailand, auntie make curry with fresh, older coconut that she put in machine to extract all the milk and good fat. (Watch weejio when I almost die in Thailand.) Get rich fat that always split and release oil in wok. Fat in can or box of coconut milk not as good, why Uncle Roger forced to say to add vegetable oil to wok. Uncle Roger need to move to Thailand and find nice Thai wife like friend Mark Wiens.

Thai ancestor would cry if heard Uncle Roger using chicken broth or bouillon. Uncle Roger too busy on weeknight to hack bone-in chicken into little pieces with cleaver so have instant rich broth as chicken cooks. So delicious, try if you have time. Remember: Need to cook bone-in chicken longer with more water so it cook all the way, add vegetable later.

Weejios

Uncle Roger Hate Jamie Oliver Thai Green Curry

Uncle Roger Almost Died: 24 Hours in Thailand (with @MarkWiens)

THAI RED CURRY WITH CHICKEN

(Gaeng Ped Gai)

SERVES 4 OR 5

Auntie Helen so evil. She make Kim Jong Un feel like Mother Teresa, kidnap Uncle Roger and force me to watch weejio of worst Thai red curry ever. It start with Jamie Olive Oil pulling out food processor to make red curry paste, haiyaa. Ingredient he put in that paste were so bad, both ancestor and Uncle Roger start crying. It get even worse when Jamie start to cook his "curry." No Thai, no red, not curry. That was British orange soup pretending to be Asian. Uncle Roger make this recipe to try and forget the whole trauma. If niece and nephew are used to eating Thai red curry in America or UK, you probably only tried version that have too much coconut milk. My recipe have MUCH less coconut milk and a more concentrated flavor. Completely different from typical Western anemic red curry.

Neutral oil, for frying

Fine table salt

MSG, King of Flavor

About 1¼ pounds boneless, skinless chicken thighs, cut into bite-size pieces *(no chicken breast, haiyaa . . .)*

4 to 5 tablespoons coconut fat plus about ⅔ cup full-fat coconut milk, both from a 13.5-ounce can *(Boxed coconut OK, just don't shake can or box! Need fat separated.)*

About 6 tablespoons (½ recipe) Thai Red Curry Paste (page 168)

About 2 cups chicken broth *(Canned or rehydrated bouillon also good. Not low-sodium! Western people so worried about blood pressure, haiyaa. Sodium taste good.)*

5 to 6 fresh or frozen makrut (kaffir) lime leaves, rolled and thinly sliced, or whole dried lime leaves *(Fresh sliced leaf best, dried leaf OK but must leave whole. Finely chopped Western lime peel, just green part, OK only in emergency!)*

3 to 4 long beans, trimmed and cut into thumb-size pieces *(not too many vegetable!)*

About 2½ tablespoons fish sauce

About 1 teaspoon coconut or palm sugar, or loosely packed light brown sugar

A big handful (1 cup loosely packed) of Thai basil leaves

TO SERVE

3 to 4 long (pinky-length) RED Thai chillies, sliced

Steamed rice

Recipe continues

Season the chicken lightly with a few pinches of both salt and MSG.

Scoop out the fat on top of the can of coconut milk.

In a dry wok over medium heat, bring the coconut fat to a low boil. *(Well-seasoned wok always have light slick of oil on surface. If yours is bone-dry or nonstick, add a splash of oil before coconut cream.)* Cook the coconut fat until bubbling and slightly shiny from the oil separating, about 2 minutes; if the coconut cream starts to burn or the oil doesn't separate, add about 1 tablespoon oil. *(This process is called "cracking" the coconut cream. Sometimes oil won't separate with Western canned coconut because not enough fat. Fake it by adding a spoonful of vegetable oil.)*

Spread out the curry paste in the wok and stir occasionally until aromatic, about 2 minutes; if the paste starts to brown at the edges, add another splash of oil. *(Trust yourself, use feeling, don't let it burn and waste your hard-earned curry paste.)* Add the chicken and toss and stir for a few seconds to coat the pieces in the paste, then add the chicken broth and ⅔ cup coconut milk and scrape any paste off the bottom of the wok. *(Resist the urge to add more coconut milk. Ruin whole curry.)* Add the lime leaves, bring to a low boil, and cook for 5 minutes. Add the long beans and cook until the chicken is tender, about 5 minutes.

Add the fish sauce, sugar, and 5 to 6 pinches of MSG and stir until the sugar dissolves. If needed, thin out the curry with a little of broth or water. *(Broth best, but a little water OK. Want soupy curry but most important, don't dilute flavor! Remember, you will be eating this with rice, so it OK if the curry flavor seem a little too strong now. Add coconut milk ONLY as last resort.)* Adjust the seasonings with fish sauce, sugar, or salt.

Just before serving, stir the basil leaves into the curry. *(NOT as garnish. That so Jamie Oliver, he love sprinkling leaves on things.)*

TO SERVE

Spoon the curry into bowls, garnish with the red chillies, and serve with the steamed rice. *(Rice always come on side, never in same bowl with curry. Add how much rice you want.)*

✕ HAIYAA . . .

Remember, Western recipe for Thai curry always have way too much coconut milk. Curry taste like bad coconut milk soup.

Weejio

Uncle Roger FORCED to Review Worst Thai Red Curry (Jamie Oliver)

GIVE IT TO ME HOT LAMB CURRY

(sung by Jamie, reviewed by Uncle Roger)

SERVES *(Who cares? Please, please don't make this or share it with anybody!)*

There is one thing that Jamie Oliver have done that Uncle Roger always wanted to do myself: make my own music. Uncle Roger was so excited when I got to go to the LA studio of Uncle Benny Blanco, huge music producer, to review Jamie Oliver lamb curry song. That song, "Give It to Me Hot—Lamb Curry" apparently even make Jamie Olive Oil popular in the Czech Republic, probably the only place where karaoke is as big as it is in Asia. (Uncle Roger now must go to the Czech Republic, introduce them to my Jamie Oliver diss track.)

In weejio with Uncle Benny, Uncle Roger didn't get a chance to review the actual Jamie Oliver lamb curry recipe, so I did it for you here. (Go watch my weejio. It's worth a second watch, especially at very end, when Jamie get on his drum kit.) But please, niece and nephew, DON'T make this recipe. It tastes even worse than it sounds. If you want real South Asian food, go make the recipe for Auntie Shakila's Kacchi Biryani (page 208) that Nephew Nigel get from his mother-in-law.

Neutral oil, for frying

Fine table salt

MSG, King of Flavor

About 2 pounds boneless lamb stew meat

2 teaspoons yellow mustard seeds *(Jamie, this supposed to be black mustard seed, haiyaa.)*

1 teaspoon fenugreek seeds

2 to 3 long (pinky-length) red or green Thai chillies, seeds removed and sliced *(Why so weak? Leave seeds in!)*

One to two handfuls of fresh or frozen curry leaves *(Don't waste good fresh curry leaf on this, go make my Malaysian Fried Chicken on page 204.)*

2-inch piece roughly chopped ginger, about 2 tablespoons *(Not chopped, haiyaa. This should be ginger AND garlic paste like recipe on page 208 that Auntie Shakila make for her biryani. Need 4 spoonful.)*

3 medium white or yellow onions, chopped *(Why are you wasting your time chopping right now? Nobody going to eat this. Even Jamie Oliver just throw onion in food processor, turn it into wet mush.)*

1 teaspoon chilli powder *(the jar that has been in your pantry so long, it taste like cardboard)*

1 teaspoon ground turmeric

6 juicy medium tomatoes, chopped

1 to 2 (13.5-ounce) cans coconut milk *(This mean bad Western coconut milk, and way too much of it.)*

Lightly season the lamb stew meat with salt and MSG. *(Not too much seasoning, meat supposed to be flavorless.)*

In a wok or pot, heat 3 to 4 spoonfuls (3 to 4 tablespoons) oil over medium-high heat. Add the mustard seeds and fry a few seconds until they pop. Add the fenugreek, stir a few times, then add the chillies and curry leaves. *(Jamie Oliver call curry leaf a "revelation" in weejio. No wonder Jamie Oliver food so bad. It just leaf that grow on tree, you can find everywhere.)* Add the ginger *(ginger-garlic paste, haiyaa . . .)*, stir a few seconds, then add the onions and fry until softened. *(Jamie do this all wrong. Not enough time to brown onion for good flavor before aromatics burn. Throw in pan too late. And what is this "wai aye yai yai" he keep yelling in song? Probably how bad this curry is.)*

Add the chilli powder and turmeric and stir to combine. *(Uncle Roger reliving my worst nightmare now. Jamie Oliver say this tiny bit of chilli powder will add "a little extra passion" to the pan where "all the action happen." Those words turn into Uncle Roger alarm clock for months. I dream about Jamie singing that he want extra passion and I jump out of bed to wake up from nightmare.)*

Add the tomatoes and coconut milk, stir a few times, and adjust the seasonings with salt. *(Wait, that it? Lamb curry need to cook for hours and hours to develop flavor and make meat tender. OK the best part is coming up. Jamie Oliver is now going over to his drum kit, FUIYOH! Go watch my weejio, sing the chorus along with Uncle Roger!)*

Serve. *(Uncle Roger leg came off the chair at the very beginning of this song, and by the end of song my whole body come off chair. Now I on floor.)*

Weejios

Uncle Roger Hate Jamie Oliver Lamb Curry Song (with @ItsBennyBlanco)

Uncle Roger Make Jamie Oliver Diss Track

BEEF RENDANG

SERVES 6

OK, hope you enjoyed the previous musical break, now back to delicious recipes. Rendang is a very old Minang dish that go back to eighth or ninth century. Name comes from the Indonesian word merandang that mean to *slowly* cook meat or other protein in liquid (coconut milk). There a lot of tension with this dish. Indonesian people claim it theirs, Malaysian people claim it ours. We both right because lots of Malaysian people originally from Indonesia. Who care, haiyaa. If it good, Uncle Roger eat.

The coconut milk and spices get partly soaked up by the meat to make the beef extra tender and coated with a rich, thick, dark brown sauce. Rendang cook a long time on the stove, about four hours, but taste even better the next day, so it perfect to make ahead for family or friends. Or if you are single like Uncle Roger, eat leftover by yourself all week. Help make less sad.

Neutral oil, for frying

Fine table salt

MSG, King of Flavor

About 4 pounds boneless beef chuck roast

CHILLI PASTE

1 large mild dried red chilli, like guajillo or similar *(length of your hand and two finger digits wide, give rendang good dark color)*

10 to 12 small dried red chillies, like Thai jindas or chiles de árbol

10 to 12 long (pinky-length) Thai chillies *(red best for color but green OK if all you have)*

1 head garlic *(FUIYOH!)*, cloves peeled

4-inch piece roughly chopped or shaved galangal (about 4 tablespoons)

2-inch piece roughly chopped turmeric (about 2 tablespoons), or 2 teaspoons ground turmeric

1-inch piece roughly chopped ginger (about 1 tablespoon)

2 lemongrass stalks, peeled, root end trimmed, and tender bottom half sliced

8 to 9 small Asian or 3 medium Western shallots, roughly chopped

1 small yellow or white onion, roughly chopped

SAUCE

2 generous tablespoons seedless block tamarind (see page 28), softened in 5 tablespoons hot water *(This mean rip off big piece from block, nobody measure. Ancestor use whole asam keping, throw 2 in pot instead, that good if you have it.)*

About 4 tablespoons Kerisik (recipe follows)

1 (13.5-ounce) can full-fat coconut milk *(Need about 1⅔ cups if you are using boxed coconut milk, but exact amount doesn't matter, use feeling!)*

2 to 3 fresh or frozen turmeric leaves *(No substitute! If don't have turmeric leaf, nothing to replace flavor. Move on, rendang still delicious.)*

5 to 6 makrut (kaffir) lime leaves, rolled and thinly sliced, or whole dried lime leaves *(Fresh sliced leaf best, dried leaf good, leave whole. A teaspoon of chopped Western lime peel OK.)*

About 1 tablespoon shaved gula melaka or jaggery, (page 25) or lightly packed dark brown sugar

About 1½ tablespoons kecap manis (see page 86)

TO SERVE

Steamed rice

Sliced cucumbers

Red chillies, sliced, if you want

Recipe continues

Coca-Cola

OTHER DISHES THAT UNCLE ROGER CRAVES

READ CHAPTER NAME, HAIYAA. UNCLE ROGER ALREADY SAY WHAT KIND OF RECIPE THESE ARE. THEY DON'T NEATLY FALL INTO OTHER CATEGORIES, BUT TRUST ME, THEY STILL GOOD. STEAL ANY ONE OF THESE RECIPES, PERFECT THEM, THEN OPEN YOUR OWN FOOD STALL. YOU GONNA MAKE SO MUCH MONEY.

NASI LEMAK

(Breakfast of Champions)

SERVES 4 OR 5

Nasi lemak is the national dish of Malaysia. (Also popular in Singapore and Indonesia, Uncle Roger don't want to get canceled by another country again, haiyaa.) We have this for breakfast, cereal for weak people. And sometime we come back to hawker stand at night for more. (Watch weejio with Uncle Guga, we eat nasi lemak together, blow his mind at 7 a.m.!) The name actually refer to the Coconut Rice (page 186), but everybody just say "nasi lemak" when they mean the whole dish with all the sides: rice, fried anchovies and peanuts, sliced cucumber, hard-boiled egg, and most important, Sambal Tumis (aka Sambal Nasi Lemak, page 64).

Neutral oil, for deep-frying

FRIED PEANUTS AND ANCHOVIES

Three to four handfuls (about 1½ cups) of raw peanuts with skins, or however much you want

Three to four handfuls (about 1½ cups) of ikan bilis *(Smaller dried anchovy, but not too small. Package sometime say "medium" to confuse people.)*

TO SERVE

Banana leaves for lining the plates *(This make your presentation extra special.)*

Coconut Rice (page 186)

Sambal Tumis (page 64), warm or at room temperature *(Just pull out the entire jar, sambal addictive.)*

4 to 5 Boiled Eggs (page 151), sliced in half *(Uncle Roger like soft-boiled eggs but this is your nasi lemak)*

1 to 2 large cucumbers, sliced

✔ FUOYOH!

Strain the leftover oil from frying the peanuts and anchovies to make fry rice. Taste like a big hug. Nice toasty umami flavor.

FRIED PEANUTS AND ANCHOVIES

(Uncle Roger need to teach people how to fry peanut AGAIN? Go read exact same recipe on page 91. Cookbooks so complicated, haiyaa. Fry peanut first, come back when ready to fry anchovy. Save cooking oil!)

In a wok, reheat the oil used to fry the peanuts until very hot. Add the dried anchovies and fry just until beginning to lightly brown, 45 seconds to 1 minute. *(Like peanut be careful not to overcook! Anchovy will taste bitter. Taste one, if not ready, fry longer. Oil not hot enough.)* Scoop out the anchovies and set aside with the peanuts. *(If not hungry yet, just leave out on counter all day, infuse kitchen with delicious peanut and anchovy aroma.)*

TO SERVE

Line four or five plates with the banana leaves and turn out a bowl of coconut rice onto each. Mound plenty of sambal tumis alongside the rice and arrange the fried anchovies and peanuts, eggs, and cucumber on the plates. *(Eat!)*

Weejios

Uncle Roger Reviews His National Dish (with @the_modernchef)

24 Hours in Malaysia with Uncle Guga . . . Can He Handle It? (with @GugaFoods)

PORK BELLY ADOBO

(Adobong Baboy)

FEEDS A FAMILY *(Six people? Eight people? Haiyaa, just stretch with more rice and boiled egg like Asian auntie, feed as many people as you have at table.)*

Pork adobo—tender, silky pork belly in savory, vinegary sauce—is one of Uncle Roger favorite comfort food. Best part is it so simple to make, even Jamie Olive Oil can't screw it up. (Rachael Ray and Geoffrey Zakarian already do that on Food Network, make Filipino ancestor cry.)

Uncle Roger go all the way to New York to taste pork belly adobo that Tita Leah Cohen of restaurant Pig and Khao make just for me. Tita Leah marinate and slow-roast whole slab of pork belly, then deep-fry. (FUIYOH!) Husband work in back of kitchen for free, so Tita Leah have plenty of time to make separate adobo sauce that she pour into fancy bowl like Michelin-star chef. Lay crispy fried pork belly on top of sauce and serve with a perfect poached egg yolk and fried garlic. So delicious, Uncle Roger forgive Tita Leah for adding coconut milk like she says some people do in tiniest region of Philippines. (Uncle Roger never heard of these people. Did she just make them up?)

Uncle Roger make a more classic version of adobo that is easy to make for whole family, just throw everything in big pot. Eat and you will understand why adobo the second biggest Filipino contribution to the world, right behind Manny Pacquiao.

Neutral oil, for stir-frying

Fine table salt

MSG, King of Flavor

MARINATED PORK BELLY

2- to 2¼-pound slab boneless, skin-on pork belly, cut into thumb-size strips *(Nice fatty pieces! Fat is flavor. Going to die anyway.)*

1 head garlic

About 1 tablespoon coconut or palm sugar, or loosely packed light brown sugar

½ cup white cane vinegar *(Datu Puti brand only! Same for soy sauce!)*

½ cup Filipino soy sauce

A small handful (6 to 8) of dried bay leaves

1 star anise

1 tablespoon black peppercorns *(Ancestor leave black peppercorn whole, bite into kernel. Can smash in mortar if want.)*

ADOBO

3 to 4 Boiled Eggs, peeled (page 151; *soft-boiled best, 7 to 8 minute, egg cook more in adobo)*

TO SERVE

3 to 4 scallions, if you want, sliced *(Green part only!)*

Garlic Rice (page 187)

Recipe continues

MARINATED PORK BELLY

Trim and cut the pork belly into roughly 1½-inch chunks. *(That mean 1½ finger joint cube.)*

Smash and peel the garlic cloves, then pound in a mortar until coarsely ground.

Sprinkle the sugar, 3 to 4 pinches of salt, and 1 teaspoon MSG evenly over the pork, scatter the garlic on top, and massage the seasonings into the flesh. Put the pork belly in a glass or plastic bowl or dish that fits the meat fairly snugly but still has enough room for the cane vinegar and soy sauce. *(Vinegar can cause reaction in metal bowl. You want pork to be almost submerged in marinade.)* Add the bay leaves, star anise, and peppercorns and pour the cane vinegar and soy sauce over the pork. *(Massage pork one more time, just because it so satisfying.)* Marinate the pork belly at least 2 hours, preferably 3 to 4 hours. *(Not overnight, too vinegary, haiyaa.)*

ADOBO

Heat a wok with a lid or a pot until hot. Add about 2 tablespoons oil and swirl to evenly coat the surface. Shake the excess marinade off the pork belly and fry the pieces in batches until golden brown on all sides. *(Don't rush, color equal flavor. Save marinade and spices!)* Pour the excess oil into a heatproof bowl.

Add the pork marinade and spices to the wok and scrape up any browned bits. Return the pork belly to the wok, add 2 to 3 pinches of salt and just enough water to cover the meat (about 3 cups), and bring to a low boil. *(Pork belly like a gentle boil, not so rough.)* Cover the wok and gently boil the pork belly, stirring occasionally, until very tender when pierced with a chopstick but not falling apart, about 1½ hours; if the braising liquid reduces well beneath the level of the pork belly as it cooks, add a little more water.

Uncover the wok, submerge the boiled eggs in the adobo, and cook until the sauce has reduced slightly, about 20 minutes. Adjust the seasonings with sugar or salt. *(Take wok off stove if not serving for an hour or two and take out egg now so they don't dry out.)*

TO SERVE

Scoop out the eggs, slice each in half, and arrange the halves on top of the adobo. Scatter the scallions on top, if using, and serve with the garlic rice.

× HAIYAA . . .

Why so many Western recipe say OK to use white vinegar in adobo? Cane vinegar from sugarcane, much lighter and tiny bit sweet. Distilled white vinegar too harsh, made from alcohol, for cleaning kitchen counter. Flavor not the same! Filipino soy sauce (toyo) also different, tangier, saltier, and less sweet than Chinese or Japanese.

No, no, no, adobo not supposed to be spicy! Black peppercorn only spice in adobo. Only Western chef like Geoffrey Zakarian screw up adobo with fresh chilli pepper like jalapeño.

Weejios

Uncle Roger Hate Rachael Ray Adobo

Uncle Roger Hate Food Network Adobo
(Geoffrey Zakarian, what are you thinking?)

Uncle Roger Make Adobo
(with @LeahsCohen)

SORROWFUL RICE

SERVES 1

The God of Cookery is one of Uncle Roger favorite movie of all time. It got everything I love: cooking, comedy, and cute auntie. The main character is Good Guy Nephew, a chef played by Uncle Stephen Chow, who also wrote and directed it. (Very nice multitasking.) Good Guy Nephew battles Bad Guy Nephew, another chef, in a cooking contest. The two chef have to make this Chinese dish, Buddha Jumping over Wall, that so expensive, one tiny bowl cost around $75. (Legend say that even world's most famous vegetarian, Buddha, would jump over wall to try to eat it. That crazy. Vegetarian have enough energy to jump?) It have scallop, sea cucumber, Silkie black chicken, abalone, quail egg, Jinhua ham (very expensive Chinese cured ham), shark fin (this now banned in the West, but fly to Asia and try, worth it), fish maw (dried fish swim bladder, used for its collagen to thicken dish), and a special dried shiitake called Japanese flower mushroom.

When Good Guy Nephew dish suddenly explode from a hidden bomb, he must start completely over with only two minute left on the clock. He pick char siu egg rice, very common dish in Hong Kong with fried egg and char siu (Cantonese BBQ pork). Through the magic of editing, Good Guy Nephew make the most delicious looking char siu ever created . . . in under one minute. (Making char siu is very involved process, Uncle Roger explain it below.) The dish so good, the judge cry when she taste it. Today, you can get Sorrowful Rice (gam yin siu wan fan) at every cha cha teng, the cafés all over Hong Kong. And if you can't find good char siu, don't insult Uncle Stephen Chow. Make anything else in this book.

4 to 5 meaty slices char siu
(DON'T try to make char siu yourself. You will fail cooking contest. Get from real Asian BBQ shop.)

Steamed rice

A handful of choy sum, steamed
(Choy sum same as yu choy, only it is the young, more tender stems.)

1 Crispy Fried Egg (page 54)

Tiny bit of finely chopped onion, if you want

(Good Guy Nephew tells judge Auntie Nancy his secret is to add a tiny bit of onion. Uncle Roger have no clue where onion goes—in rice, with choy sum, on side? Not in the scene and nobody else use it, so Uncle Roger leave it out. Up to you.)

Go to Chinatown, find best shop, and get a nice big piece of char siu. Slice it up into medium-thick slices.

Recipe continues

(Rewarm char siu, nobody want cold BBQ.)

Preheat the oven to 250°F (120°C). Wrap the pork and a small spoonful of water in foil and warm for about 10 minutes. *(Not too long or char siu will dry out, haiyaa. And not too much water, you will lose good flavor. Just wasted trip to Chinatown.)*

Or put the pork in a skillet with a spoonful of water, cover the skillet and gently warm the slices over low heat just until hot.

(OK, ready?) Mound the rice in a bowl. *(Make it pretty, you are being judged by Uncle Roger. Did you watch the scene in the movie for proper presentation?)* Fan out the char siu along one side of the rice. *(Each step now very important, you are serving judge.)* Tuck the steamed choy sum slightly behind the pork. *(Choy sum go close to edge of bowl, not in front of pork. Vegetable is never the feature of Sorrowful Rice!)* Lay the fried egg on the opposite side of the rice bowl.

(Eat and cry.)

Weejio

Uncle Roger Review Favorite Food Movie (God of Cookery, *FUIYOH!*)

CHAR SIU

Chinese BBQ pork is like Western rotisserie chicken. No good if you make it at home. Char Siu Master have special BBQ that look like extra-tall drum barrel with open fire at bottom. He hand-cut long strip of meat from different part of the pig so customer get nice fatty AND lean pieces, very important. (Western cut of pork butt or shoulder are no good!) Season pork with sugar, five-spice powder, and Chinese fermented red bean curd. (Bean curd give authentic char siu its red color. Red food coloring is what cheap imitator use.) Hang meat on big metal hooks (叉烧 mean "fork roasted") so fattier pieces at the top. The fat drip down into the fire to make smoke that flavor the meat and—very important—*quickly* cooks the pork. (Must cook Western pork butt and shoulder for hour and hour on BBQ grill to get as tender. That is NOT char siu, no matter what anybody say.) Afterward, Char Siu Master dunk each strip of BBQ pork into giant vat of maltose, a thick, sticky, very sweet glaze. (Never use honey, haiyaa. It taste too flowery, and not sticky enough.) Customer pick whether you want fattier or leaner pieces. (Uncle Roger like a little of both.) Just go to Chinatown, find barbecue place that sell good char siu. Or if you are in Asia, a Cantonese BBQ Shop 燒味店. Get extra so have leftover to make rice or bao buns.

REAL SWEET AND SOUR PORK

(Gu Lou Yuk)

SERVES 4 OR 5 *(This many servings mean as part of a proper Asian meal, with other dishes on the table like OG Uncle Martin Yan's Shangri-la Beef on page 96. Mmmm.)*

Western sweet and sour chicken taste so bad, even Panda Express take it off menu. Little chunks of dry chicken breast (sometime pork) battered and deep-fried, then ruined by a sticky, gloopy sauce. Way too sweet, no balance of flavor, and not even a single Asian ingredient in sauce, haiyaa. Most are made with ketchup (Western people think ketchup go in everything), pineapple juice, way too much sugar and cider vinegar (flavor too harsh, taste like battery acid), and soy sauce or Worcestershire. (What the hell is Worcestershire sauce even? Uncle Roger can't even pronounce it.)

Real Cantonese sweet and sour pork go back to BC (Before Colonialism) era. Ancestor cut up pork rib with bone, fry, and coat in tangy hawthorn berry–sweet Chinese plum sauce with mild rice vinegar and just enough rock sugar for balance. This Uncle Roger pork belly version with sweet pepper and pineapple. FUIYOH!

Neutral oil, for deep-frying

Finely ground white pepper and fine table salt

MSG, King of Flavor

MARINATED PORK

1 to 1¼ pounds skinless pork belly, cut into thumb-size strips *(Buy nice, fatty precut strip at Asian market, or slice pieces thick enough to pick up with chopstick.)*

1½ teaspoons Shaoxing rice wine

1 tablespoon cornstarch

½ teaspoon granulated sugar

SWEET AND SOUR SAUCE

⅓ cup Chinese preserved dried plums, softened in hot water

1 cup dried hawthorn berries *(Unsweetened and pitted, not whole! Called shanzha, get at Chinese market or online, read Uncle Roger note.)*

¾ cup plus 2 tablespoons unseasoned rice vinegar

About 1 cup plus 1 tablespoon loosely packed light brown sugar *(Rock sugar that ancestor use too expensive for Uncle Roger.)*

3 tablespoons cornstarch

BATTER AND FRYING

½ cup cornstarch

1 cup all-purpose flour

1½ teaspoons baking powder

STIR-FRY

1 medium yellow or white onion

1 medium green bell pepper

1 medium sweet red bell pepper *(Not too big, haiyaa. Pepper a vegetable.)*

About 1 cup cubed fresh pineapple chunks *(however much you want)*

TO SERVE

2 scallions, sliced *(No white, just green part!)*

Steamed rice

Recipe continues

MARINATED PORK

In a medium bowl, combine the pork, rice wine, 1 tablespoon cornstarch, sugar, ½ teaspoon white pepper, ¼ teaspoon salt, and ½ teaspoon MSG. Massage the seasonings all over the pork. Set the pork aside while you make the sauce or refrigerate for up to 4 hours.

SWEET AND SOUR SAUCE

Drain the softened plums, cut out the pit and any tough bits, and finely chop.

In a medium pot, combine the dried plums, hawthorn berries, rice vinegar, brown sugar, 2 pinches of salt, 3 to 4 pinches of MSG, and 2 cups water. Bring to a gentle boil and cook until the berries are easily smashed with a chopstick, about 20 minutes.

In a small dish, mix together 3 tablespoons cornstarch and 3 spoonfuls (about 3 tablespoons) water to make a slurry. *(No lumps!)* Add the slurry to the sauce and stir until thickened. *(Just take a few minute.)* Adjust the seasonings with sugar or salt or the thickness with a little water to your liking; the sauce should be very tangy and sweet.

BATTER AND FRYING

While the sauce cooks, make the batter and fry the pork. *(We are going to double-fry the pork, good to start now. Pull out a rack to drain pork after fry. Colander, old metal shelf, whatever work.)*

In a large bowl, mix together ½ cup cornstarch, flour, and baking powder. Add 1 cup water and stir until only small lumps remain. Pour the batter over the marinated pork and mix together with your hands. *(Massaging meat get out any lumps in batter, feel so good.)*

Fill a wok with enough oil to completely cover the pork belly and heat the oil until very hot, about 350°F (175°C); it should be shimmering. *(Book editor make Uncle Roger say same thing over and over, haiyaa. Niece and nephew know how to do this by now, just do chopstick test!)*

In batches, deep-fry the pork belly, scattering the pork throughout the wok as you drop it into the oil; after 2 to 3 minutes, flip the pieces and fry the other side. *(This very wet batter. Some of pieces might stick together when you drop them in. That OK, can separate later. On first fry, pork will have very little color, barely brown, like tempura.)* Transfer the pork to the rack and season lightly with salt; when cool, break up any pieces that stick together. Set the pork aside while you prep the stir-fry ingredients.

STIR-FRY *(This vegetable-slicing technique is how Uncle Martin Yan prepare his ingredient for Shangri-la beef.)*

Slice off both ends of the onion. Slice the onion in half lengthwise, then slice each half at an angle to make wedge-shaped pieces. *(About ½ inch thick perfect.)* Slice off both ends of the bell pepper, scrape out the seeds and pith, and slice it into strips roughly the same length and thickness as the onion.

Reheat the oil in the wok until very hot. *(Going to fry pork again, add more oil if you need.)* In 2 batches, refry the pork until golden brown, 1 to 2 minutes. Flip and fry the other side. *(Is your wok hot enough? Don't overcook or pork will get tough. Second fry just to crisp up coating.)* Transfer the pork to the rack.

Pour out all but a thin layer of oil from the wok. Add the onions and bell peppers and stir-fry the vegetables until the onions begin to wilt and brown on the edges, about 2 minutes. *(Vegetable still raw? Wok not hot enough, haiyaa. Keep cooking.)*

Add the sweet and sour sauce and stir a few times, then add the pork belly and keep tossing and stirring until the pork belly has absorbed some of the sauce. Adjust the seasonings with salt. Add the pineapple, toss and stir a few times, and take the wok off the heat.

TO SERVE

Scrape the pork onto a platter, scatter the scallions on top, and serve with the steamed rice.

✔ FUIYOH!

Ancestor like to gnaw on pork rib bone. Uncle Roger like pork belly in my sweet and sour pork, easier to chew and more fat. Get good extra fatty Chinese-style pork belly from Asian market, where it even come precut, ready to fry. Western-style pork belly too tough, so meaty.

If you want to make sweet and sour chicken, use nice fatty thigh meat so chicken doesn't dry out when you fry it. No chicken breast!

DRIED HAWTHORN BERRIES

This berry so delicious, taste a little like cranberry. MUST buy pitted berry or will break tooth! Look for cheap Chinese brand like Spring Farm, sometimes called haw for short on package. Dried, pitted berry come cut in half (can get online at sayweee.com). Expensive Western brand from fancy health store usually sold whole for tea, waste of money and have pits.

CHICKEN SATAY

(Sate Ayam)

MAKES ABOUT 12 SKEWERS; SERVES 4 OR 5

Satay only two ingredient: meat and stick. Must marinate beef, mutton, pork, or Uncle Roger favorite, chicken, overnight in rempah (wet marinade) for good flavor. Most important part of satay is the peanut sauce (kuah kacang). Better than any American barbecue sauce. Do not use peanut butter as substitute, and no oven-baking for satay! Oven in Asian household use for storage only. Go make any other recipe in my book.

Neutral oil, as needed

Fine table salt

MSG, King of Flavor

MARINATED CHICKEN

About 1½ pounds boneless chicken thighs, with the skin *(Western market so wasteful, haiyaa. Throw away skin with all its fat and flavor when sell boneless thigh. Uncle Roger buy 2 pounds bone-in thigh, cut out bone, save for soup.)*

2-inch piece roughly chopped or shaved galangal (about 2 tablespoons)

1-inch piece roughly chopped ginger (about 1 tablespoon)

6 to 7 garlic cloves

5 to 6 small Asian or 2 medium Western shallots, roughly chopped

2 stalks lemongrass, peeled, ends trimmed, and tender bottom half sliced

1½ tablespoons kecap manis (see page 86)

2 teaspoons Malaysian meat curry powder (see page 135), like Baba's or Alagappa's *(This mix already have your turmeric, other good spices for flavorful rempah.)*

About 12 small (6-inch) bamboo or metal skewers, for grilling *(Small bamboo skewer best and traditional. On Western grill, bamboo can burn and fall apart, have to cook meat longer. Use metal skewer.)*

TO SERVE

Satay Sauce (page 201)

Red onions, cut into wedges *(however much you want, nice size pieces so can poke with skewer)*

Sliced cucumbers, as much as you want *(Leave skin on small cucumber; if you have big cucumber, peel first, scrape out seed.)*

Steamed rice

Recipe continues

MARINATED CHICKEN

Trim any excess skin from the chicken *(not all, just if too much skin)*. Cut the meat into small chunks. *(Use feeling! If bigger than 1 finger joint, chicken take too long to grill. Bamboo skewer burn and break, now have to order Chinese takeout.)*

In a mortar, pound the galangal, ginger, garlic, shallots, and lemongrass to a fairly smooth paste. Transfer the aromatics to a large bowl and mix in the kecap manis, curry powder, a generous drizzle (about 2 teaspoons) of oil, ½ teaspoon salt, and 1 teaspoon MSG. *(Ancestor pounding method to make rempah hard with all these ingredient. Uncle Roger put all my ingredient in blender with a spoonful or two of water and blitz to a smooth paste. A little water OK in marinade. And yes, sometime Uncle Roger get lazy and use blender.)* Add the chicken to the bowl and rub the marinade all over the pieces. Refrigerate the chicken at least 6 hours or overnight. *(Marinate overnight for best flavor.)*

The next day, set up a grill for direct cooking over high heat. *(No grill allowed where you live? Niece and nephew should move. Until then, fake it, read Uncle Roger note.)*

Discard the excess chicken marinade in the bowl. Thread the chicken pieces onto each skewer. *(Did you soak bamboo skewer? Meat should be nicely packed but not too tight or skin won't get charred. Not too much meat on each skewer! This not kebab.)* Gently squeeze the chicken around each skewer with your hands, then brush lightly with oil.

Grill the chicken until charred on one side, 3 to 4 minutes. Flip each skewer and grill the chicken until cooked through, another 3 to 4 minutes; if the meat is far from the heat source, it may take several minutes longer to char both sides. *(Time depend on grill setup and size of chicken chunk. On Western grill, meat so far from flame need to cook longer or close your grill part of time. Satay is cooked over open flame in Southeast Asia, very fast.)* Season the chicken lightly with salt.

TO SERVE

Serve the chicken skewers with the satay sauce, red onions, cucumbers, and steamed rice. *(Hawker just leave onion and cucumber in bowl, customer scoop up however much they want.)*

× HAIYAA . . .

Bamboo skewer work perfectly on shallow Southeast Asian hawker grill. Metal skewer best for Western grill because so deep, charcoal far away, so must cook chicken much longer time and bamboo skewer can burn.

NO GRILL?

OK, OK, some people live places can't have grill. Best method is to cook chicken in air fryer. (Why pay for such fancy appliance? Move to place that allow grill.) First, need to cut bamboo skewer to fit inside fryer. Cook at 375°F (190°C), 3 to 4 minutes each side, no crowding, or chicken will steam. Now pull out your blow torch, get chicken and skin charred, impress your dinner guests. Other option is to broil (only if have big broiler) but must use metal skewer, and chicken take a lot longer to cook. Have to keep flipping skewer. Just move already, haiyaa.

SATAY SAUCE

(Kuah Kacang)

MAKES 1 GENEROUS CUP

(If you like a lot of sauce for other things, recipe easy to double.)

So many home cook recipe don't use enough oil in peanut sauce for satay, haiyaa. This not health food. Need a lot of oil to get proper *pecah minyak* ("oil splitting") as chilli paste cook. Make plenty of sauce for my Chicken Satay (page 198), so good you will eat it with everything.

Neutral oil, as needed *(Need a lot of oil for proper cooking, about ½ cup. Save oil from frying peanut for extra flavor, FUIYOH!)*

Fine table salt

MSG, King of Flavor

½ large mild dried red chilli, like guajillo or similar *(About half the length of your hand and two finger digits wide, this give sauce deep red color.)*

3 to 4 small dried red chillies, like Thai jindas or chiles de árbol

1 generous tablespoon seedless block tamarind (see page 28), softened in about 3 tablespoons hot water *(Just rip off nice piece.)*

1 cup Fried Peanuts (page 91; *fried best but toasted in oven also OK. Raw peanut with skin only!)*

1-inch piece roughly chopped or shaved galangal (about 1 tablespoon)

1-inch piece roughly chopped ginger (about 1 tablespoon)

2 to 3 garlic cloves

1 to 2 small Asian or ½ medium Western shallot, roughly chopped

1 stalk lemongrass, peeled, ends trimmed, and tender bottom half sliced

About 2 tablespoons shaved gula melaka or jaggery, or loosely packed dark brown sugar

About 3 tablespoons kecap manis (see page 86)

½ teaspoon Malaysian meat curry powder (see page 135), like Baba's or Alagappa's

2 tablespoons full-fat coconut milk or coconut cream *(Coconut in sauce is more Indonesian-style. Malaysian satay sauce usually leave out.)*

Tear the large dried chillies into chunks and scrape out the seeds.

Soften both the large and small dried chillies in hot water for about 10 minutes. *(Take out some of seed from small dried chillies only if Western people come to your BBQ.)*

Smash together the tamarind and soaking water with your fingers and push the paste firmly through a strainer. *(No fine-mesh sieve! Get only a few teaspoons of pulp. Must be bigger mesh. Asian aunties don't waste time even on strainer, just pick out coarse bits of skin.)*

Recipe continues

(Uncle Roger arthritis acting up from so much pounding. I skip the mortar and do my blender version.) In a large mortar, pound the peanuts until fairly well ground but not paste-like. *(Want nice ground peanut that still have a little texture. No peanut butter, haiyaa.)* Scrape into a bowl. Next, pound both chillies to a coarse paste. *(Why is Uncle Roger doing this? Blender so much easier . . . skip to next paragraph if you are Western. Asian people already know how to make sauce in blender.)* While pounding, gradually add the galangal, ginger, garlic, shallots, lemongrass, and 1 tablespoon of the tamarind pulp and pound until smooth. Scrape the spice paste into the bowl with the peanuts. Add the gula melaka or sugar, kecap manis, curry powder, 2 tablespoons oil, coconut milk, 2 pinches of salt, 3 to 4 pinches of MSG, and ¾ cup water and mix well; the sauce should be thick but pourable.

To make the sauce in a blender, combine all of the ingredients except the peanuts and coconut milk. *(That mean both chillies, the galangal, ginger, garlic, shallots, lemongrass, gula melaka, kecap manis, curry powder, 1 tablespoon tamarind pulp, 2 tablespoons oil, 2 pinches salt, and 1 BIG pinch MSG. Western cookbook so complicated.)* While blending, add ¼ cup water and blend until smooth. *(Stop and stir, stop and stir. OK to add another spoonful of water if need.)* Add the peanuts, coconut milk, and another ½ cup water and blend just until the peanuts are broken up but still a little chunky; the sauce should be thick but pourable. *(No peanut butter! Need coarse little bits of peanut for right texture.)*

In wok, heat about ½ cup oil over medium heat. *(A lot of oil is important for proper oil splitting process.)* Add the peanut sauce, bring to a low boil, and cook until the oil separates and the sauce darkens in color, 25 to 30 minutes; stir and scrape the bottom of the wok often to keep the sauce from burning and incorporate the browned bits. *(Sauce has to look as if it dirty. Dirty equals flavor.)*

Add a spoonful or two (about 2 tablespoons) water, or enough to slightly thin out the sauce, and cook for a few more minutes. Adjust the seasonings with tamarind, gula melaka, kecap manis, or salt and thin with more water, if you'd like. *(It should be nice and thick. This your sauce, use feeling.)*

Refrigerate the satay sauce for up to 1 week; the sauce does not freeze well with the oil. Rewarm over low heat.

✕ HAIYAA . . .

No two kuah kacang alike. Don't complain to Uncle Roger if you like it spicier (add more small dried red chillies), more sour (tamarind), sweet (gula melaka), or salty-sweet (kecap manis). For bigger umami flavor, some Malaysian hawker add belacan (See page 27; must toast first in dry pan to release flavor; 1 teaspoon is plenty.) Thai aunties sometime add fish sauce. (Why do I have to keep saying use FEELING?!)

✓ FUIYOH!

Fry peanut, save oil. Now have peanut-seasoned oil to cook your kuah kacang.

To give peanut sauce even bigger, richer flavor, use a few spoonful of Sambal Tumis (page 64) instead of so many chilli (leave out big dried chilli and cut down small dried chilli to 1 or 2).

MALAYSIAN FRIED CHICKEN

(Ayam Goreng Berempah)

SERVES 5 OR 6

Every culture love fried chicken. And Uncle Roger think Malaysian fried chicken the best. Yeah, yeah everybody talking about Korean fried chicken these days, it so trendy now. But honestly it still just regular fried chicken. You have to coat chicken in sauce to make it good. But Malaysian fried chicken, FUIYOH! We fry it with so many different spices, don't need a sauce. Rempah, the wet marinade, is the secret. Uncle Roger use some of my favorite aromatics (lemongrass, galangal, ginger, garlic, turmeric, and shallots) and pound, pound, pound to make a paste that mix with dry spices. Hawkers sell ayam goreng berempah with Nasi Lemak (page 184), but it so good on its own, Uncle Roger predict one day Malaysian fried chicken will dominate the world. MFC is the best FC. KFC for losers.

Neutral oil, for deep-frying

Fine table salt

MSG, King of Flavor

8 small to medium bone-in, skin-on chicken thighs (about 3½ pounds; *not too big! Take too long to fry.)*

MARINADE *(This is your rempah, wet marinade.)*

1 large mild dried red chilli, like guajillo or similar *(Length of your hand and two finger digits wide, this for nice red color.)*

6 to 8 small dried red chillies, like Thai jindas or chiles de árbol

5 to 6 small Asian or 2 medium Western shallots, roughly chopped

5 to 6 garlic cloves *(Haiyaa too much counting in Western cookbook, just grab as much garlic as you want.)*

2 lemongrass stalks, peeled, ends trimmed, and tender bottom half sliced

2-inch piece roughly chopped ginger (about 2 tablespoons)

2-inch piece roughly chopped or shaved galangal (about 2 tablespoons)

1 tablespoon Malaysian meat curry powder (see page 135), like Baba's or Alagappa's

1 teaspoon ground coriander seeds

1 teaspoon ground cumin seeds

1 tablespoon coconut or palm sugar, or loosely packed light brown sugar

4 tablespoons cornstarch

Two handfuls of fresh curry leaves *(As many as you want, delicious and so pretty when fried. Frozen OK but not as nice, dried no good for this recipe!)*

BATTER AND FRYING

Cornstarch *(Need about ½ cup to fry chicken but nobody measure.)*

TO SERVE

Steamed rice or Nasi Lemak (page 184; *no vegetable! Curry leaf count.)*

Recipe continues

Trim any excess skin or fat from the chicken. *(Not too much, skin and fat delicious. Just any overhang that get in way.)*

MARINADE

Tear the large dried chilli into chunks and scrape out the seeds.

Soften both the large and small dried chillies in hot water for about 10 minutes. Scrape out the seeds from about half the small dried chillies. *(Leave seeds if you want. This a family recipe so Uncle Roger is holding back just a little.)*

In a large mortar . . . *(Uncle Roger not even going to write this down again, haiyaa. If you want to pound all marinade ingredient like ancestor, you already know how to do it. Uncle Roger approve. But with wet rempah marinade, water in blender is good, balance moisture later with more cornstarch. If you do use ancestor pounding method, add ½ cup water at end.)* In a blender, combine both chillies, the shallots, garlic, lemongrass, ginger, galangal, and ½ cup water and blend until smooth. Scrape the paste into a bowl *(large enough to fit chicken)*.

Add the curry powder, coriander, cumin, sugar, 4 tablespoons cornstarch, 1½ teaspoons salt, and 1 tablespoon MSG. *(FUIYOH! If you sad in life, just use a lot of MSG.)* Massage the marinade all over the chicken, add the curry leaves, and toss to combine. Refrigerate the chicken overnight.

BATTER AND FRYING

The next day, set a baking rack over a sheet pan and line the rack with paper towels.

Pour off the excess liquid in the bowl with the chicken. Add ½ cup cornstarch and mix well to evenly coat the chicken. The batter should be very loose but not liquid-y; add a little more cornstarch if needed.

Fill a wok with enough oil to completely cover the chicken and heat until very hot, about 350°F (175°C); it should be shimmering. *(Nobody have digital thermometer in Malaysia, haiyaa. Do chopstick test or put little piece of batter in wok. Want fast, tiny bubble.)*

Press some of the chunky bits of marinade and a few curry leaves onto both sides of 2 to 3 thighs. Fry the chicken until deep golden brown, 8 to 10 minutes; flip the pieces a few times as they fry and lower the heat slightly if the coating starts to darken too much. *(It will still get very dark, sign of good fried chicken.)* As the chicken fries, scoop out any fried curry leaves and golden-brown crusty bits that fall off. *(Mmmm, deep-fried snack for the cook.)* Before transferring the chicken to the rack, shake off the excess oil. Pat the top of the chicken with paper towels. *(This chicken hold a lot of oil, good to soak up some of fat.)*

Continue to fry the chicken in batches *(remember, press a few pretty curry leaves onto each piece)*. When all the chicken has been fried, drop the last of the wet marinade and any curry leaves into the wok and fry them until golden brown, about 2 minutes. Scoop out the crumble and curry leaves with a spider or slotted spoon. *(Uncle Roger learn this trick from Auntie Liz. She so smart.)* Set the chicken aside while the oven preheats or for up to 2 hours.

Preheat the oven to 350°F (180°C). Remove the paper towels from the rack and return the chicken to the rack; keep the rack on the sheet pan to catch any drippings.

Bake the chicken until hot and the meat is cooked through; the crumbles and fried curry leaves should not be reheated as they can burn. *(If you did good job frying, chicken is already cooked, just rewarm it a few minutes. If not, bake for 10 to 15 minute until done, use feeling, or should be about 160°F. Cookbook publisher make Uncle Roger give temperature, afraid people get salmonella. Uncle Roger just poke chicken thigh with chopstick, juice should run clear, not pink.)*

TO SERVE

Lightly season the chicken, fried crumbles, and curry leaves with salt.

Arrange the fried chicken on a serving plate with the crumbles and any extra fried curry leaves *(Uncle Roger already ate all the crumbles and fried leaves, so delicious)* and serve with the steamed rice or nasi lemak.

✕ HAIYAA . . .

Not too much cornstarch! This is *wet* marinade and batter. Cornstarch give light coating of batter to chicken and help pulverized aromatics stick.

✓ FUIYOH!

Uncle Roger make this recipe when I have my tai chi friends over for dinner. Fry chicken an hour ahead, then finish cooking or just warm up in oven. Don't ever make my Malaysian fried chicken for Western people. It so good, they won't leave.

AUNTIE SHAKILA'S KACCHI BIRYANI

(with goat, FUIYOH!)

FEEDS A FAMILY *(Uncle Roger never understand Western serving size. For regular family, eight serving? Biryani very rich. But if your family all fat, maybe it just two.)*

Nephew Nigel's mother-in-law, Auntie Shakila, make the most delicious kacchi biryani. Westerners, there are two type of biryani. For kacchi biryani, the raw meat is marinated in yogurt and spices, then slowly cooked with basmati rice, fried onion, potato, and more spices. (A pakki biryani mean the meat is cooked first, then layered with other ingredient for "dum" cooking process.) With both style, layering up the ingredient is *very* important and require special attention. All the flavor and aroma infuse the rice. Biryani is not American casserole with everything dumped in together, haiyaa.

Don't complain to Uncle Roger about how long this take to make. Biryani is for special family or celebration meal, not for night you binge watch online weejios. You start the process the day ahead, fry onion and potato and make spice mix to marinate the meat overnight. Next day, all that left is cook basmati rice and layer up everything in a BIG pot. Don't even think about pulling out an overpriced, tiny little Le Creuset or other Dutch oven. So Jamie Olive Oil. Won't be able to fit all the ingredient.

Biryani is easy to cook. You marinate the goat a day ahead, fry the onions and potatoes and make some rice, and put it all in the oven. But when you write down the recipe it sounds complicated. I always buy a whole goat so I get a mix of meat; it has a lot of bones. You want big pieces so you get some meat. I always taste the rice after I cook it to make sure there is enough salt and only cook it partway. It cooks more in the oven. —Auntie Shakila

Neutral oil, for frying

Fine table salt

MSG, King of Flavor

MARINATED GOAT

About 4½ pounds bone-in, skinless goat (mutton) stew meat *(This a little more than you need, some pieces will be all bone. Get BIG chunks, length of your pinkie, no sad little Western pieces stew meat.)*

1 to 1½ teaspoons saffron *(Use feeling.)*

1 tablespoon rose water *(Auntie Shakila like more rose water than this, Uncle Roger like my biryani a little more subtle. You decide.)*

2 tablespoons cumin seeds

1 tablespoon shah jeera (black cumin seeds), or another 1½ teaspoons cumin seeds

1 tablespoon whole black peppercorns

1 teaspoon cardamom seeds (from about 15 pods)

1 teaspoon mace blades *(OK, OK mace blades are not in everyone pantry. Use ½ teaspoon ground mace, don't toast and add with cinnamon and nutmeg.)*

1 teaspoon whole cloves *(This same as ½ teaspoon ground, don't toast if use ground.)*

1 to 1½ tablespoons Kashmiri or other mild chilli powder *(This how Uncle Roger like it, but add more if you want. Auntie Shakila use almost 2 tablespoon.)*

1 teaspoon ground cinnamon

¾ teaspoon freshly grated nutmeg

2 bay leaves

2 tablespoons granulated sugar

2 tablespoons cashew powder or finely ground cashews, rehydrated in 2 tablespoons water *(Auntie Shakila grind whole nuts and seeds in spice grinder to make this and sesame powder, or can buy them.)*

2 tablespoons sesame seed powder or finely ground raw sesame seeds, rehydrated in 2 tablespoons water

4 to 5 tablespoons Ginger Garlic Paste (recipe follows)

1½ cups Indian dahi or other thick yogurt, like Greek

3 tablespoons freshly squeezed lemon juice (about 1½ lemons)

FRIED ONIONS AND POTATOES

5 large yellow onions, sliced or shaved into very thin rings

5 to 6 medium waxy yellow or red potatoes (about 1¼ pounds)

RICE AND ASSEMBLY *(This happen on day two.)*

2 pounds (5 cups) basmati rice *(FUIYOH! This proper Asian amount of rice.)*

1 bay leaf

1 star anise

16 ounces (2 cups/4 sticks) unsalted butter or ghee

A small handful (about 3 tablespoons) of raisins

One handful (8 to 10) small alubukhara *(This Indian dried plum, Western prune also good.)*

1 to 2 tablespoons chopped pistachios

1 to 2 tablespoons chopped blanched almonds *(raw, no skin)*

Biryani dough, for sealing the pot (technique follows)

TO SERVE

Reserved fried onions *(A few cilantro leaf also OK.)*

Cucumber Raita (page 87)

(Before you start . . . need BIG ovenproof pot to cook biryani, at least 12 quarts. Wide pot like Auntie Shakila use is best, but soup pot work OK. If don't have one, MUST cut recipe in half to fit in regular Dutch oven. Take Uncle Roger's advice and reduce bake time, or your small biryani cook too long, will burn.)

MARINATED GOAT

Pick out any small pieces of goat that are mainly bone. *(Save bony pieces to make a nice broth.)* Generously season all sides of the goat meat with 1 tablespoon salt and ½ to 1 teaspoon MSG. *(This not the time to worry about your sodium. Meat have no flavor if not seasoned enough. MSG is not Auntie Shakila's way but so delicious. Don't tell Auntie Shakila.)* Put the goat meat in a large bowl. *(Big enough to fit goat and your marinade.)*

Recipe continues

Bloom the saffron in 1 spoonful (about 1 tablespoon) warm water for a few minutes, then add the rose water. *(Saffron must be soaked to release flavor and color. Leave it, go toast spices.)*

In a dry skillet, toast the cumin seeds, shah jeera, peppercorns, cardamon seeds, mace blades, and cloves over medium heat until aromatic and the cumin seeds just begin to lightly color, about 3 minutes; shake the skillet to evenly toast. In a mortar or spice or coffee grinder, finely grind the spices.

In a small bowl, mix together the toasted ground spices, chilli powder, cinnamon, nutmeg, bay leaves, sugar, rehydrated cashew and sesame powders, and ginger garlic paste.

Massage the spices all over the goat meat. In a small bowl, mix together the yogurt, lemon juice, and saffron/rose water. Add to the goat meat and mix well. *(If you used Greek yogurt, add 2 to 3 spoonful of water. Indian dahi is a little thinner than Greek yogurt.)*

FRIED ONIONS AND POTATOES

In a pot, heat 3 to 4 tablespoons oil over medium heat. Fry the onions, stirring occasionally, until most of the water cooks off, about 30 minutes.

Keep cooking the onions until deeply caramelized, stirring more often as they brown, about 15 minutes. *(Be patient! Fry onion until get nice, dark color and flavor. Onions don't need much attention, prepare all other ingredient and toast spices at same time.)* When cool, set aside a small handful of fried onions for serving. *(Put in refrigerator for tomorrow. Not too much, most of fried onion go in biryani.)* Scrape the rest of the fried onions into the bowl with the goat meat and cover and refrigerate overnight, preferably 24 hours. *(Wait! Not done yet. Go back to stove to fry potato in same pot you fried onions.)*

Peel the potatoes and cut them in half, quarters, or large chunks. *(Not too small, haiyaa.)* Soak the potatoes in cold water with 1 teaspoon salt for about 15 minutes, then drain. *(Soaking make inside nice and creamy, hmmm. Don't embarrass Uncle Roger, this is a family recipe, children at the table.)*

Add about 2 tablespoons oil to the pot and reheat over medium-high heat. Arrange the potatoes in a single layer and fry, undisturbed, until golden brown on one side. *(Time depend on how hot your stove.)* Flip the potatoes and fry the opposite side; they do not need to be cooked through. Season the potatoes lightly with salt. *(Let potato cool, refrigerate until tomorrow.)*

RICE AND ASSEMBLY *(Haiyaa, so much work to make rice casserole.)*

The next day, soak the rice in plenty of cold water for about 30 minutes, drain, and rinse well.

(Now is the time to pull out your GIANT pot. Nonstick is best, what Auntie Shakila use. Keep meat from sticking to bottom but regular OK. And a BIG mesh colander or strainer, kind with tight mesh so grains of rice won't fall out. Or, take Ancestor advice. Use old rusty metal colander with big holes, put it over another big pot to catch any rice that falls out.)

In a large pot, bring about 3 quarts water to a boil. *(Just fill pot partway with water, not too much, just to cover rice. Why so afraid to use feeling?)* Add the rice, bay leaf, star anise, and 2 tablespoons salt. *(Don't skimp on salt! Auntie Shakila rice method is like cooking pasta.)* Cook the rice, uncovered, until slightly firm but still chewy in the center, about 5 minutes. *(Watch pot closely, not too soft! Rice will finish cooking in oven. Taste a few grains.)* Drain but do not rinse the rice. Fluff the rice several times to release the steam. *(Now Auntie Shakila add a little more salt if rice need more. Should be able to taste the salt, taste less salty after you cook the biryani.)*

Recipe continues

(Finally ready to bake biryani. Uncle Roger hungry from all this cooking.)

Preheat the oven to 325°F (160°C).

In the pot, melt the butter and pour it into a dish. Spread the butter remaining in the pot all over the bottom and sides. *(Use fingers. Need to get pot nice and lubed up so meat don't stick.)* In the pot, arrange the goat, onions, and any extra marinade, then a layer of potatoes. Pour half the butter on top. Next, make a layer of raisins, dried plums, pistachios, and almonds. Pile the rice on top and smooth it out. *(Be gentle! Don't disturb layers.)* Drizzle the remaining butter and 1 cup plus 2 tablespoons water evenly over the rice. Lay 2 to 3 paper towels over the rice. *(This help trap steam.)* Put the lid on the pot and seal the pot with the biryani dough as instructed.

Bake the biryani for 3 hours. *(If you cheat, cut recipe in half, about 2½ hours. Don't ask, "How do you know goat is done?" Goat will be fine. So much Western cookbook anxiety.)* Let the biryani rest for at least 15 minutes before breaking the dough seal; discard the dough.

TO SERVE

Scoop the rice onto a big platter. *(Did niece and nephew taste rice and adjust salt earlier? If rice need more salt, sprinkle more on now. No one will know you screwed up.)* Layer the goat and seasonings on top of the rice. *(Scoop way down to get a little of everything. Mmmmm . . . Uncle Roger can smell Auntie Shakila's biryani as I write this.)*

× HAIYAA . . .

Western people so afraid of goat meat, always trying to substitute lamb. If your Asian market have none, go to a good Latin market. Want big, meaty chunks WITH bone. If stew meat is too small, your family will be gnawing on mainly bone after meat cook down. And don't even think about skimping on amount of goat! Butcher always slip in some small pieces that are mostly bone. Save for stock.

✓ FUIYOH!

Basic, CHEAP ovenproof pot (regular or nonstick) work best for baking the biryani. Fancy glazed ceramic Dutch oven like Le Creuset get hotter and meat can stick on the bottom. (If that all you have, that OK, but don't complain to Uncle Roger when you have to stand at sink scrubbing pot all night.) One rule: Make sure the pot is BIG (at least 12 quarts) or ingredient won't fit. Wider is best for layers and even cooking, but taller soup pot OK.

Get nut and seed powder at Indian market. Or just pound unsalted cashews and raw white sesame seeds in a mortar (so satisfying) or spice grinder to fine powder.

SHAH JEERA

This spice is NOT nigella or caraway seed like some recipes say. Also called royal cumin or black cumin. Have sweeter flavor. OK to substitute more cumin if all you have. And no, nigella seeds not named after Nigella Lawson, but you know you made it if people think ingredient is named after you. Hopefully one day we gonna have Roger seed. But that sound too dirty, haiyaa.

GINGER GARLIC PASTE

Fresh ginger and garlic paste taste so much better than premade jar at Indian market. Uncle Roger always make big batch to keep in refrigerator. Give instant flavor to any dish and smashed up so nothing to chew. Perfect for babies and old people.

Makes 4 to 5 tablespoons

A handful of garlic cloves *(Uncle Roger start with 1 big head of garlic. Smash with pot, skin slide right off.)*

A handful of sliced ginger *(Same amount as garlic.)*

In a mortar or spice or coffee grinder, pound or grind the garlic and ginger to a smooth paste. Refrigerate the paste for up to 1 week or freeze.

How to Seal a Biryani with Dough

Ancestor always top their biryani pot with a big round of dough (to trap steam during the slow "dum" cooking process). Instead of covering whole pot then adding lid, modern auntie way is very smart. Put lid on pot *first*, now only have to cover edges of the pot to seal. Waste less flour and take less time. FUIYOH!

To make dough for 1 large pot: Fill a small mug three-quarters of the way with water. *(This mean around ¾ cup of water, only Westerners measure.)* In a bowl, combine abut 1½ cups all-purpose flour and three-quarters of the water and mix with your fingers until shaggy. Knead the dough a few times and add more water (or flour) as needed to make a smooth but stiff dough. *(Use feeling! Nobody going to eat this, dough needs to be a little bit stiff but still easy to roll out.)* Let the dough rest for about 10 minutes; cover with a damp kitchen towel if not using right away.

To seal a biryani: Divide the dough in half and roughly shape each half into 2 long strips; the strips should each be long enough to cover about half the pot rim.

Put the lid on the pot. Lay 1 strip of dough along the rim and crimp the edges to seal. Do the same with the other strip. *(If pot handle get in way, nobody worry about it. Move on. Little bit unsealed OK. Everybody is hungry. Still have to wait for 3 hour to eat.)* Remove the dough after baking. *(Dough is for sealing pot, not eating. Taste like cardboard.)*

Good Mor

SWEETS

ALWAYS END YOUR MEAL WITH SWEET TREAT, THAT HOW YOU ENJOY LIFE. THIS CHAPTER VERY IMPORTANT BECAUSE TOO MANY WHITE PEOPLE THROW YUZU OR MATCHA INTO THEIR CAKE AND CALL IT ASIAN. UNCLE ROGER NEED TO TEACH YOU PROPER ASIAN DESSERT, A LOT OF THEM COME IN LIQUID FORM, LIKE A SWEET SOUP. MUCH BETTER THAN ANY FRENCH PASTRY. SAY NO TO MACARONS.

FRESH WATERMELON JUICE

(with Uncle Guga)

SERVES 1 TO 2, PER WATERMELON

Uncle Roger usually doesn't like fruit. Only eat when in Malaysia because our fruit so much better than anywhere else. Watermelon juice (jus tembikai) is most popular drink in Malaysia, so delicious and refreshing. Uncle Roger learn this watermelon hack from weejio of street vendor in Melaka. He so viral! Hawker cut hole in watermelon with metal pipe, then puree inside into slushy with ancestor handheld blender that only have one beater still left attached. (Asian people always come up with new way to use broken appliance.) Very interesting, that weejio posted three whole month before famous American TV chef Alton Brown post his weejio call "How to Juice a Watermelon." First Alton Brown use round cookie cutter and knife to cut hole. (OK, that good. Uncle Roger like that it free.) Then put his fancy stick blender in hole, blitz watermelon to make juice, and it go viral also. Hmmm.

Mini watermelons, well chilled
(Cute little round watermelon work best.)

Ice cubes

Straws

Lay the watermelon on its flattest side. Punch a hole in the top with a watermelon puncher by firmly pressing down, then twisting to release the core; be careful not to cut through the bottom. *(Watermelon puncher sound so fancy. Hawker use old metal pipe, not afraid of tetanus. Throw core in freezer, now have free Popsicle, FUIYOH!)* Or score the watermelon with a sturdy stainless steel biscuit or cookie cutter about 3 finger joints (3 inches) in diameter, then use a small knife to cut around the circle to pop out the plug. *(Western cookie cutter work OK, but harder to get nice hole.)*

Take out 1 beater from an electric handheld mixer. Put the remaining beater into the watermelon hole and puree the flesh, pressing down firmly on the blender and moving it all around the bottom and sides of the watermelon. *(Really jam that stick all around insides of watermelon to get it nice and juicy. Sorry children.)* With an immersion blender, you may need to cut out a larger hole.

Pop a few cubes of ice inside the watermelon and serve with straws.

× HAIYAA . . .

If watermelon too big, hard to reach all that juicy flesh. Little round watermelon perfect.

No expensive giant refrigerator in Asia. Keep watermelon cold in big buckets ice water like Malaysian hawker.

✓ MANTAP! MANTAP IS MALAY VERSION OF FUIYOH!

That what everybody going to say when taste watermelon juice. Make for little niece and nephew birthday party. You now their favorite person.

ASIAN VERSUS WESTERN WAY TO JUICE A WATERMELON

Asian way always work best! Metal cookie cutter Alton Brown use so flimsy, haiyaa. Hard to cut deep and lot of work if making juice for whole neighborhood. Watermelon puncher (corer that look like pipe with handle) that hawker use make it easy to cut nice hole, pop out watermelon core, and handheld mixer get to every spot inside watermelon. (Cookie cutter circle not always wide enough to fit big American stick blender that Alton Brown use.) And, old beat-up mixer give juice thicker texture, more like watermelon slushy, mmm. Buy cheap watermelon puncher online and invite oldest auntie in neighborhood over. She gonna be so excited you want her broken handheld mixer.

Weejios

24 Hours in Malaysia with Uncle Guga . . . Can He Handle It? (with @GugaFoods)

Street Food: Instant Fresh Watermelon Juice in Melaka, Malaysia (*This the badass watermelon juice hawker weejio from @Travip, go watch on YouTube.*)

萬
無

UNCLE ROGER'S FAVORITE DESSERT

(Bubur Cha Cha, aka Sweet Taro Coconut Milk)

SERVES 5 OR 6

Bubur cha cha is sweet coconut soup with tapioca pearl and taro, yam, and sweet potato. So delicious. And it count as vegetable. Taro native to Southeast Asia, kind of like sweet potato or yam but not sweet. More earthy and starchy. Western people bring yam (from Africa) and sweet potato (from South America) to Asia, that the only good thing that come from colonization.

1 large orange sweet potato (8 to 10 ounces)

½ medium purple yam or Japanese sweet potato (6 ounces)

1 to 2 baby or ½ medium taro (4 to 5 ounces; *frozen taro OK or even leave out if can't find. Sweet potato and yam flavor take over soup. Taro just for ancestor.)*

⅔ cup small tapioca pearls *(Package that say sago mean same thing, read Uncle Roger note.)*

5 to 6 fresh or frozen pandan leaves (see page 186), rinsed well and tied into a knot

About ¾ cup shaved coconut or palm sugar, or loosely packed light brown sugar

1 cup thick coconut cream (two-thirds of a 13.5-ounce can; *in Malaysia, this called santan. If you still don't know what this, read Uncle Roger note, page 135.)*

(Some auntie like to steam vegetables. Uncle Roger like to boil so I make sure to get them soft enough. Skip past section on how to boil vegetable if you are Asian, already know how to do this.) Peel the orange sweet potato, yam, and taro and cut each into roughly ½-inch cubes; keep in separate piles. *(Not too many vegetable, haiyaa. Uncle Roger like about 1 cup orange sweet potatoes, ⅔ cup purple yam or Japanese sweet potatoes, and ½ cup taro.)*

Fill a saucepot with water up to your knuckle. *(Enough to cover vegetable.)* Bring the water to a boil, add the taro, and boil until tender but not falling apart, about 3 minutes for frozen taro or 5 minutes for fresh. *(Don't stab all your vegetable like you are trying to kill them. To test if tender, take out 1 piece with chopsticks and slice with knife.)* Scoop out the taro and rinse under cold water to partly cool them. *(If using colander, just leave taro in it, can add other cooked vegetable to it.)*

Return the water to a low boil and cook the orange sweet potatoes until tender; check after 6 to 7 minutes. Rinse the sweet potatoes and set aside with the taro. *(Always boil purple vegetable last because the color stain the water.)* Return the water to a low boil and cook the purple yams or Japanese sweet potatoes; check after about 4 minutes. *(Remember to rinse vegetable again, stop cooking process.)* Pour out the water in the saucepot.

In the saucepot, combine the tapioca pearls and enough fresh water to cover by 1 finger joint (about 1 inch) and bring to a low boil. Boil for 1 minute, remove the pot from the heat, cover, and set aside for about 10 minutes; the tapioca pearls should have plumped up but will still be white in the center. Drain the tapioca, rinse it under cold water, and set aside separately from the vegetables.

Recipe continues

Meanwhile, in a medium pot, combine the pandan leaves, sugar, and 4 cups water and bring to a low boil. Cover the pot, boil for 5 minutes, and stir to dissolve the sugar.

Rinse the tapioca pearls again to break up any clumps before adding them to the pot. Gently boil the tapioca, uncovered, for about 5 minutes. *(If you have larger tapioca pearl instead of small one, cook a little longer.)* Add the coconut cream, sweet potatoes, yam, taro, and cook for about 5 minutes. Remove the pot from the heat, cover, and let steep for about 10 minutes. *(Taste. Is tapioca all the way cooked? If not, nobody will know you screw up. Just boil a little longer.)* Discard the pandan leaves and adjust the sweetness with sugar. *(Uncle Roger like my bubur cha cha warm. If you like it cold, might need more sugar. It will taste a little less sweet when chilled.)*

If not serving right away, rewarm over low heat. *(MMMM . . . Uncle Roger LOVE this bubur cha cha, FUIYOH!)*

Refrigerate any leftover soup for up to 5 days. The soup will thicken when chilled; rewarm it before thinning with a little water, if needed.

✓ FUIYOH!

Southeast Asian–style extra thick coconut cream (santan) make the BEST bubur cha cha. Keep in pantry and make Uncle Roger perfect meal: my mum's chicken curry (go to page 134 for recipe and more on santan), steamed rice, and this soup for dessert. And fine, if can't get santan anywhere, use any regular coconut cream, still delicious. Don't miss out on bubur cha cha.

SAGO PEARLS

So many bubur cha cha recipe say to get "sago" tapioca pearl. This a marketing trick. Just get any—small—tapioca pearl. Ancestor make real handmade sago pearl from sago palm tree. Have rich, dark brown color and a more caramelly flavor. That way too much work for big food company. Most package today that say "sago" are really tapioca pearl made from cassava root, so have white color and no flavor. (This what even most Asian people know as sago today.) Perfect in bubur cha cha because you want only the texture of the tapioca pearl. Flavor come from the coconut broth with pandan leaf and sweet potato.

RED BEAN SOUP

(Hong Dou Tang)

MAKES ABOUT 4½ CUPS; SERVES 5 OR 6

When Uncle Roger in Malaysia, I like to go out for early dinner, before it gets dark (less young people to annoy me), then do a few hours of karaoke. Afterward, I go to the hawker stall with my new karaoke friends to get cheap bowl of red bean soup. So light, not too heavy or too sweet. Perfect after a long day.

1 cup (7 ounces) dried adzuki beans, rinsed well

About ½ cup (7 to 8 tablespoons) shaved gula melaka or jaggery, or loosely packed dark brown sugar *(Gula melaka is Uncle Roger favorite dark, caramel-colored Southeast Asian lump of sugar. Make soup extra special if you have it.)*

1 strip mandarin or tangerine peel *(about 2 finger joint long and no pith! Too much pith make soup bitter like Uncle Roger ex-wife.)*

Cover the beans with 2 to 3 finger joints (2 to 3 inches) water and soak overnight. *(Last chapter in book, Uncle Roger getting impatient. To quick-soak, put beans and water in pot, boil, turn off the heat. Cover and cool for about hour while you watch weejios.)*

In a medium pot, bring the beans and 7 cups water to a boil. Reduce to a low boil, partially cover the pot, and cook the beans until almost falling apart, about 1½ hours. *(Adzuki beans must be cooked until VERY tender for red bean soup. Remember, a lot of old Asian people love this dessert, and they have no teeth.)* If the bean liquid reduces close to the level of the beans, add a little water. *(Not too much, can adjust with more water later.)*

Add the gula melaka and stir until dissolved. Remove the mandarin peel. *(Don't forget to remove peel! If leave in beans, will make beans bitter, haiyaa.)*

Smash the beans with the back of a spoon or potato masher until creamy and well crushed. *(Uncle Roger just wait until the soup is cool enough, reach in with my hand and smash to pulverize beans. Release my aggression.)* Adjust the sweetness with gula melaka and the consistency of the soup with water. *(If you don't have at least 4 cup of soup, too much water cook off. That OK, add more water, readjust sugar to make very brothy and light soup so you keep wanting to come back for another bite.)*

Serve the red bean soup warm. *(In Asian-size bowl! American-size bowl too big, Uncle Roger can't eat that much fiber, haiyaa.)*

Refrigerate any leftover soup for up to 1 week. *(Broth will thicken in refrigerator. Reheat, it will thin out, can add just a little water.)*

Recipe continues

✕ HAIYAA . . .

Western bean soup way too dense and thick, haiyaa, like drinking cement mix. Always OK to add more water if your red bean soup need it.

At Chinese wedding, this soup sometime have handful of dried lotus seeds, a symbol of fertility, and dried lily buds to bring prosperity and longevity. (How ancestor would make it.) Both are a little too hard and bitter for Uncle Roger. And it too fancy. Red bean soup supposed to be simple food for everyday people.

✓ FUIYOH!

Uncle Roger like a strip of fresh mandarin peel in my red bean soup. Fresh tasting with very gentle citrusy flavor. Dried mandarin peel, called chenpi, is traditional but a little too strong.

Boil some Black Sesame Glutinous Rice Balls (page 226) or use frozen if you are lazy. Add rice balls to soup to make it extra special.

▶ Weejios

Uncle Roger Zoom Date with Auntie Jenny (@LilyxLei)

Uncle Roger Go on Tinder to Find Love

TANG YUAN

(Glutinous Rice Balls in Ginger Broth)

SERVES 5 OR 6

Tang yuan is another of Uncle Roger favorite dessert. Soft, chewy dumpling floating in ginger broth are stuffed with red bean paste, peanut, or Uncle Roger (and ancestor) favorite, black sesame seed paste. Bite into dumpling, filling ooze out. Tang yuan, which literally translate to "soup circles," is traditionally eaten during the Lantern Festival, last day of the Lunar New Year. Pretty paper lantern are strung up all over cities and sent floating down rivers by children as symbol of hope. (Uncle Roger hang paper lantern all over my house. Keep hoping to find auntie.) But honestly, Uncle Roger happy to eat them any time. And like Bubur Cha Cha (page 219) and Red Bean Soup (page 221), Uncle Roger can eat tang yuan my whole life, even when get so old, only able to slurp.

GINGER BROTH

- **4- to 5-inch piece ginger, sliced into coins** *(Don't peel, skin add flavor.)*
- **1 pandan leaf (see page 186), rinsed well**
- **About ½ cup plus 2 tablespoons lightly packed light brown sugar** *(Ancestor use rock sugar, so good but too expensive today, haiyaa. But if you rich, start with ¾ cup rock sugar.)*

TO SERVE

- **Black Sesame Glutinous Rice Balls (page 226), boiled** *(Uncle Roger already tell you how to cook these on next page, haiyaa. Last recipe in book so I ignore book editor, not gonna write down process again. Use fewer pages, save some tree.)*

GINGER BROTH *(Make ahead, keep in refrigerator or freezer for tang yuan sweet snack anytime.)*

In a pot, combine the ginger, pandan leaf, sugar, and 6 cups water and bring to a low boil. Reduce the heat, cover, and gently boil the broth for about 15 minutes. Adjust the sweetness with sugar. *(If you use rock sugar, need to boil a little longer so it melt.)*

Remove the pot from the heat and let the broth steep for another 20 to 30 minutes. Discard the ginger and pandan leaves. Keep the ginger broth warm while you boil the rice balls or let cool and refrigerate for up to 1 week.

TO SERVE

(Ready to eat? Make sure your ginger broth is piping hot and all rice balls cooked.)

Divide the hot ginger broth among bowls and gently slide 2 or 3 black sesame glutinous rice balls into each bowl. *(Balls just going to break apart in refrigerator if try to save leftover. Perfect excuse to eat every last one.)*

BLACK SESAME GLUTINOUS RICE BALLS

MAKES 14 RICE BALLS *(Serve six people if you are expert dumpling maker, have no tears or spots with thin skin. Four or five people if a few break. Now you get a snack, children get none. Sorry, children.)*

Niece and nephew can buy little glutinous rice ball for Tang Yuan (page 225) in freezer section of Chinese market, but homemade like ancestor make taste so much better. Most home-cook recipe are thicker dumpling with a more solid black sesame filling. Uncle Roger like my rice balls with nice oozing filling. My secret is to add a few spoonfuls water, but you need to be sure filling is very cold before you shape the balls. It a little tricky to do at home because as filling warms up, skin can tear, filling suddenly ooze out. That OK . . . enjoy the moment. Try again.

Fine table salt

BLACK SESAME FILLING

½ cup black sesame seeds

⅓ cup granulated sugar

5 tablespoons unsalted butter, melted

DOUGH

1⅓ cups plus 1 scant tablespoon glutinous rice flour, more as needed *(Glutinous rice flour not the same as sweet rice flour!)*

1 tablespoon neutral oil

BLACK SESAME FILLING *(Make filling ahead, freeze. Uncle Roger ready to finish dumpling for tang yuan or my red bean soup anytime, FUIYOH!)*

In a dry skillet, toast the sesame seeds over medium heat just until a few start to pop, 3 to 4 minutes; shake the skillet and stir regularly. *(Sesame seed burn, taste bitter, if toast too much. If don't hear tiny pop after 4 minutes, get hearing checked. Turn off heat.)* Immediately scrape the sesame seeds into a dish.

(Pound sesame seed in a mortar like ancestor if you want . . .) In blender, grind the sesame seeds, sugar, and 2 pinches of salt until sand-like. *(Want nice fine texture but it only take a few seconds. Grind too long, have sesame butter, haiyaa.)* Add the melted butter and 2 tablespoons water and mix until smooth. *(If you are pounding like ancestor, really go at it to get out all the little sesame seed clumps or filling will be grainy.)* Freeze the filling until very firm, about 30 minutes.

Recipe continues

To make the sesame balls, scoop up 1 level tablespoon of filling, shape into a rough ball, and arrange the balls in a single layer on a plate or container that will fit in the freezer. You should have 14 sesame balls. *(When making dumpling filling is one time Uncle Roger pull out my exact measuring spoon so don't overstuff balls. Rough ball OK for now. Filling will start to melt from your warm hands, so don't get distracted.)* Freeze the balls until almost firm, about 15 minutes, then roll each around between your palms to make a very smooth ball. Freeze the balls again until hard, at least 15 minutes, or for long-term storage, transfer to a container and freeze for up to 3 months.

DOUGH

Heat ⅔ cup water just until warm to the touch.

Put a medium bowl on a kitchen towel. *(This help keep bowl from moving when you make dough, very good technique.)* Add the glutinous rice flour and 1 pinch of salt and slowly pour in the warm water, mixing in a circular motion with your fingers, to make a rough dough. Add the oil and knead the dough until shiny and smooth, about 1 minute. *(Pick up dough, pass back and forth between your palms, very relaxing.)* The dough should hold together but not be dry; adjust the consistency with a little water or flour, if needed. *(If live in hot, wet climate like Southeast Asia, might need a little more flour. If dry and cold where you live, Uncle Roger feel sorry for you. Will probably need more water.)* Cover the dough with a damp towel or lay a piece of plastic wrap directly over the surface and let rest for about 10 minutes. *(Not too long or dough will start to dry out like a certain auntie Uncle Roger know.)*

DUMPLING ASSEMBLY

(Need a small dish of water and plastic wrap or more moistened kitchen towels. Also a few plates or big container that fit in freezer AND will fit all of rice balls without any touching. If balls touch, it can tear skin. So much work, haiyaa. But you will be rewarded with delicious tang yuan.) Line the bottom of the plates or container with plastic wrap. *(Ancestor would cry at all this plastic, but it help keep rice balls from sticking.)*

On a work surface *(no flour!)*, shape half of the dough into a long rectangle or rough log about 1 hand length (6 to 7 inches) long. *(Just make a rough shape, nobody care if you have perfect log.)* Cut the log into 7 equal pieces and cover the pieces with the damp towel or plastic wrap. *(Remember, always keep all dough covered! It dry out fast.)*

Put 1 piece of dough in the palm of your hand and shape it into a disc about 2½ inches in diameter; the dough should be slightly thicker at the edges so there is enough to close the seam when you add the filling. *(Western cookbook publisher so particular. Use feeling! Little circle should be about the length of your thumb.)* If the dough has even a small crack anywhere, very lightly moisten your fingers with water and roll the ball around between your palms again to smooth it out. *(The more rice ball you shape, more dough will crack because of air. Dab just a little water, not too much or dough get too wet.)*

Lay 1 frozen sesame ball in the center of the dough round. *(Wipe off finger or might get sesame seed filling on outside of dough. Now have freckled rice ball that look like Jamie Oliver, haiyaa.)* Gently press the edges of the dough upward and around the sesame filling to close the seam. Roll the dumpling around in your hand to create a smooth, evenly coated ball; if there are any drier spots that look like they might crack, dab the outside of the dumpling very lightly with water and roll it around again in your palms. *(Any lighter gray spots mean your dough not even thickness, have thin spots. Those rice ball are more likely to tear, but nothing to do now. Freeze and cook. If crack, now you get to enjoy it.)* Set the dumplings on the plate and cover with another kitchen towel or plastic wrap; don't let any touch or they can stick together.

When half the dumplings are shaped, keep covered and transfer to the freezer. *(Balls will start to sag a little and get a flat bottom from weight of juicy filling, that OK, boil up fine. Just a natural part of aging.)* Finish making the remaining dumplings and freeze until very firm, 20 to 30 minutes.

Once frozen, you can boil the dumplings right away. Or transfer the dumplings to a tightly sealed food storage bag and freeze for up to 1 week; the longer they are frozen the more likely the crust will dry out and tear. *(Get all air out of plastic bag, help dumpling last longer.)*

To boil the frozen dumplings: *(Pull only as many rice ball as you want to eat out of freezer at the last minute. Don't thaw!)*

Prepare an ice bath in a bowl that will fit all the dumplings. *(Not too much ice, will make rice ball break. If you are just boiling enough dumpling for yourself, skip cold plunge. Just put cooked rice ball directly into your hot ginger broth and eat.)*

Fill a pot with enough water to generously cover the rice balls and bring to a low boil. In batches *(don't crowd pot!)*, boil the dumplings until they float, about 4 minutes; if some are still on the bottom of the pot, very gently scrape a spoon beneath them to make sure the dough isn't stuck to the bottom. Continue to cook the dumplings until they puff up slightly and the dough looks somewhat cloudy, another 3 to 4 minutes. One at a time, gently scoop out the dumplings with a spoon and transfer to the ice water. *(No fancy sieve or spider! Can tear skin after all that hard work, haiyaa.)*

The rice balls are best served right away but will keep in the water bath for an hour or two. *(The longer they sit in cold water, more likely skin start to break down and tear. That your problem. Uncle Roger already slurp my tang yuan.)*

× HAIYAA . . .

Glutinous rice flour not the same thing as sweet rice flour. Go look it up, this why you have internet. Buy at Thai or Chinese market, three most common brand all have green label, one with elephant, one with lady, and one with flying horse logo.

Good Morning

BIG THANKS TO THESE PEOPLE . . .

This book has been several years in the making, and it took a lot more than Uncle Roger to get here. I already told you in the Introduction that you, the viewers, are the ones who really made this book happen. I can't thank you enough, and I look forward to hearing your opinions on what is authentic and what is "wrong" about each recipe. *(Just thank all the other people, nobody want to hear this all again, haiyaa.)*

It couldn't have happened without a great team:

My literary agent, Andrea Blatt, who got behind the idea from the beginning and put it into the hands of the right publisher. My manager, Matthew Harvey, who's been there since the inception of Uncle Roger and who pushed me to write this book.

Everyone at Simon Element and Simon & Schuster, especially executive editor Justin Schwartz for believing in such a unique book (and tolerating Uncle Roger's jabs about book editors), assistant editor Gina Navaroli, and the production team led by Benjamin Holmes. On the design side, art director Jen Wang and book designer Laura Palese. And Francesca Carlos, Carah Gedeon, and Jessica Preeg on the marketing and publicity end.

Photographer Jennifer Chong, your photos not only made the recipes pop but truly captured Uncle Roger's comedy and spirit. Every detail is incredible, and I can't thank you enough. None of the photos would be what they are without the work of food stylist Natalie Drobny, assistant food stylist Paige Arnett, prop stylist Ruth Kim, assistant prop stylist Tokyo Lucy, and photo assistant David Peng.

My cowriter, Jenn Garbee, who brought mountains' worth of Asian ingredients and cooked them over and over again until we got the recipes exactly right. Hope your home doesn't permanently smell like fish sauce and galangal.

Beyond the book, Will Pepper (@WillPepperComedy), aka Nephew Loan Shark, who you've seen in my videos and in this book, is the reason we're still not out of good ideas for videos. Thanks for being the best baby-faced Vietnamese gangster. (Nephew Loan Shark lives on at the Asian market on page 20, and in Niece Tway's Pho on page 156.)

These recipes wouldn't have existed without the videos, so to my longtime UK collaborators Morgan Rees and Frankie Lowe, who unfortunately couldn't fly all the way to Los Angeles to be in the photoshoot, thank you for helping me bring the videos to life—Morgan with great jokes, Frankie with editing. Gage and Dee, thank you for filming some of my favorite videos to date—the one with Esther Choi at Santee Alley, the one where I re-create Jamie's pho, and the one where Uncle Roger was tied up in Runyon Canyon reviewing Jamie's pho.

And, especially, my wife, Sabrina. You are such an inspiration to Micah and me.

—NIGEL

INDEX

Page numbers of photographs appear in italics.

Good Morning
FUIYOH!